THE DOG BENEATH THE SKIN

or

WHERE IS FRANCIS?

THE DOG
BENEATH
THE SKIN

or

WHERE IS FRANCIS?

a play in three acts by
W. H. Auden
and
Christopher Isherwood

faber and faber

LONDON · BOSTON

First published in 1935 by
Faber and Faber Limited
3 Queen Square London WC1N 3AU
First Faber Paperback edition published in 1968
Reissued in 1986

Printed in Great Britain by
Whitstable Litho Ltd, Whitstable, Kent
All rights reserved

ISBN 0 571 08520 2

To

ROBERT MOODY

Boy with lancet, speech or gun
   Among the dangerous ruins, learn
From each devastated organ
   The power of the genteel dragon.

The first performance of this play was given in January 1936 by the Group Theatre under the direction of Mr. Rupert Doone.

DRAMATIS PERSONAE

Principal Characters

The Vicar of Pressan Ambo
General Hotham
Mrs Hotham, his wife
Miss Iris Crewe, of Honeypot Hall
Sir Francis Crewe, Bart: her brother
Alan Norman
First Journalist (*The Evening Moon*)
Second Journalist (*The Thunderbolt*)

Minor Characters

Curate	Sorbo Lamb
Mildred Luce	Chimp Eagle
H.M. The King of Ostnia	Sir William Spurgeon, the
H.M. The Queen of Ostnia	Surgeon
Grabstein, a Financier	Madame Bubbi

Destructive Desmond

Others

Bus Conductor. Hotel Porter. Village Chemist. Scout-Master. Master of Ceremonies. Poet. Cabaret Announcer. Head Waiter. Art Expert. Hotel Manager. Barman. Chorus Girls. Courtiers. Diners. Doctors. Dressers. Invalids. Lunatics. Nurses. Police. Priests. Procurers. Prostitutes. Students. Waiters. Villagers.

Two Lovers
Two Touts

9

CHORUS

The Summer holds: upon its glittering lake
Lie Europe and the islands; many rivers
Wrinkling its surface like a ploughman's palm.
Under the bellies of the grazing horses
On the far side of posts and bridges
The vigorous shadows dwindle; nothing wavers.
Calm at this moment the Dutch sea so shallow
That sunk St Pauls would ever show its golden cross
And still the deep water that divides us still from Nor-
    way.
We would show you at first an English village: You shall
    choose its location
Wherever your heart directs you most longingly to look;
    you are loving towards it:
Whether north to Scots Gap and Bellingham where the
    black rams defy the panting engine:
Or west to the Welsh Marches; to the lilting speech and
    the magicians' faces:
Wherever you were a child or had your first affair
There it stands amidst your darling scenery:
A parish bounded by the wreckers' cliff; or meadows
    where browse the Shorthorn and the maplike Fri-
    sian

As at Trent Junction where the Soar comes gliding; out
    of green Leicestershire to swell the ampler current.

Hiker with sunburn blisters on your office pallor,
Cross-country champion with corks in your hands,
When you have eaten your sandwich, your salt and
    your apple,
When you have begged your glass of milk from the ill-
    kept farm,
What is it you see?

I see barns falling, fences broken,
Pasture not ploughland, weeds not wheat.
The great houses remain but only half are inhabited,
Dusty the gunrooms and the stable clocks stationary.
Some have been turned into prep-schools where the diet
    is in the hands of an experienced matron,
Others into club-houses for the golf-bore and the top-hole.
Those who sang in the inns at evening have departed;
    they saw their hope in another country,
Their children have entered the service of the suburban
    areas; they have become typists, mannequins and
    factory operatives; they desired a different rhythm
    of life.
But their places are taken by another population, with
    views about nature,
Brought in charabanc and saloon along arterial roads;
Tourists to whom the Tudor cafés
Offer Bovril and buns upon Breton ware
With leather work as a sideline: Filling stations

Supplying petrol from rustic pumps.
Those who fancy themselves as foxes or desire a special
    setting for spooning
Erect their villas at the right places,
Airtight, lighted, elaborately warmed;
And nervous people who will never marry
Live upon dividends in the old-world cottages
With an animal for friend or a volume of memoirs.

Man is changed by his living; but not fast enough.
His concern to-day is for that which yesterday did not
    occur.
In the hour of the Blue Bird and the Bristol Bomber,
    his thoughts are appropriate to the years of the
    Penny Farthing:
He tosses at night who at noonday found no truth.

Stand aside now: The play is beginning
In the village of which we have spoken; called Pressan
    Ambo:
Here too corruption spreads its peculiar and emphatic
    odours
And Life lurks, evil, out of its epoch.

LEADER OF SEMI-CHORUS I.
            The young men in Pressan to-night
                Toss on their beds
            Their pillows do not comfort
                Their uneasy heads.
            The lot that decides their fate
                Is cast to-morrow,

> One must depart and face
> Danger and sorrow.

VOICES.   Is it me? Is it me? Is it ... me?

LEADER OF SEMI-CHORUS II.

> Look in your heart and see:
> There lies the answer.
> Though the heart like a clever
> Conjuror or dancer
> Deceive you often into many
> A curious sleight
> And motives like stowaways
> Are found too late.

VOICES.   What shall he do, whose heart
> Chooses to depart?

LEADER OF SEMI-CHORUS I.

> He shall against his peace
> Feel his heart harden,
> Envy the heavy birds
> At home in a garden.
> For walk he must the empty
> Selfish journey
> Between the needless risk
> And the endless safety.

VOICES.   Will he safe and sound
> Return to his own ground?

LEADER OF SEMI-CHORUS II.

> Clouds and lions stand
> Before him dangerous
> And the hostility of dreams.

14

Oh let him honour us
Lest he should be ashamed
In the hour of crisis,
In the valleys of corrosion
Tarnish his brightness.

VOICES.   Who are you, whose speech
Sounds far out of reach?

BOTH LEADERS [*singing*].

You are the town and we are the clock.
We are the guardians of the gate in the rock.
The Two.
On your left and on your right
In the day and in the night,
We are watching you.

Wiser not to ask just what has occurred
To them who disobeyed our word;
To those
We were the whirlpool, we were the reef,
We were the formal nightmare, grief
And the unlucky rose.

Climb up the crane, learn the sailor's words
When the ships from the islands laden with birds
Come in.
Tell your stories of fishing and other men's wives:
The expansive moments of constricted lives
In the lighted inn.

But do not imagine we do not know
Nor that what you hide with such care won't show

15

At a glance.
Nothing is done, nothing is said,
But don't make the mistake of believing us dead:
    I shouldn't dance.

We're afraid in that case you'll have a fall.
We've been watching you over the garden wall
    For hours.
The sky is darkening like a stain,
Something is going to fall like rain
    And it won't be flowers.

When the green field comes off like a lid
Revealing what was much better hid:
    Unpleasant.
And look, behind you without a sound
The woods have come up and are standing round
    In deadly crescent.

The bolt is sliding in its groove,
Outside the window is the black remov-
    ers van.
And now with sudden swift emergence   [surgeons
Come the woman in dark glasses and the humpbacked
    And the scissor man.

This might happen any day
So be careful what you say
    Or do.
Be clean, be tidy, oil the lock,
Trim the garden, wind the clock,
    Remember the Two.

ACT I

SCENE I

[*The garden of the Vicarage at Pressan Ambo. The scene suggests the setting of a pre-war musical comedy. The stage is crowded with villagers of all classes, who promenade to the strains of a distant band. The characters, as they pass in turn along the footlights, address the audience.*]

VICAR.   Here come I, the Vicar good
           Of Pressan Ambo, it's understood;
              Within this parish border
           I labour to expound the truth
           To train the tender plant of Youth
              And guard the moral order.

CHORUS.   With troups of scouts for village louts
           And preaching zest he does his best
              To guard the moral order.

GENERAL. General Hotham is my name.
           At Tatra Lakes I won my fame,
           I took the Spanish Lion.
           In Pressan now my home I've made
           And rule my house like a brigade
              With discipline of iron.

CHORUS.   Side by side his peacocks stride:

17

He rules them all at Conyers Hall
    With discipline of iron.

GENERAL'S WIFE.
              Woman, though weak, must do her part
              And I who keep the General's heart
                  Know well our island story
              And do my utmost to advance
              In India, Russia, Finland, France,
                  The just and English glory.

CHORUS.   With subtle wile and female smile,
              With speech and vote she will promote
                  The just and English glory.

IRIS.   And here am I, Miss Iris Crewe,
              I live in Pressan Ambo too,
                  The prize at village dances.
              From Honeypot Hall, the haunt of doves,
              In my blue Daimler and white gloves
                  I come to take your glances.

CHORUS.   With nose and ear and mouth and hair
              With fur and hat and things like that
              She takes our loving glances.

VICAR [*to* CHOIRBOYS].
              Well, Ernie, how's your mother? Good.
              I hope you're behaving as you should?
              Jerry, you've got a dirty face;
              Go and wash. Then we'll have a race.

1ST VILLAGER. Brazen! I should think she is!
              She doesn't care who sees them kiss,
              Can't even trouble to draw the blind.
              She's a trollop to my mind.

18

2ND V. The brooder's really excellent.
I rear now 98 per cent.
I have a new batch out to-day:
Leghorns, for I find they pay.

3RD V. I shan't mind if they choose me.
There's lots of places I want to see:
Paris, Vienna, Berlin, Rome.
I shouldn't be sorry to leave the home.

4TH V. Roll the pieces then in flour
And stew them for at least an hour,
Put some nutmeg in the pot
Garnish with parsley and serve hot.

3RD V. Perhaps they will, you never know;
What will you do if you have to go?

2ND V. There's money to be made in sheep;
Only you mustn't go to sleep.

4TH V. A glass of stout before the meal
Is always a good thing, I feel.

VICAR [*starting the race*].
Are we ready? Now Chubb, don't cheat!
Behind the line and touch your feet.

1ST V. No wonder they have had a quarrel,
The Continent is so immoral.

4TH V. Be very careful how you add the salt.

1ST V. Well, anyway, it's not his fault.

3RD V. After eight years, it seems absurd.

VICAR. Ernie first, Chubb second, Pring third.

1ST V. That dance at least should have opened his
eyes.

2ND V. Roger's heifer won first prize.

1st V.   She's carrying on with Fred.

Vicar.   Run up!
         You'll beat him yet!

4th V.   This cider-cup
         Is good.

2nd V.   Ten shillings profit on the porks.

3rd V.   Chimp Eagle.

4th V.   Recipe from wireless talks.

1st V.   Someone ought to.

2nd V.   Well, we can't complain.

Vicar. Caught you, my lad!

3rd V.   He'll be lost again.

1st V.   You saw her.

Vicar.   Clever boy!

2nd V.   It's sold.

4th V.   Taste it.

3rd V.   Choose someone.

1st V.   He's too old.

2nd V.   Barley.

3rd V.   The Choice.

Vicar.   Your legs.

1st V.   Her name.

Vicar. Jolly!

4th V.   Roasted.

3rd V.   The Hall.

1st V.   The shame.

4th V.   Ursula.

3rd V.   Saxifrage.

2nd V.   Wyandottes.

Vicar.   Game!

20

2ND V. He didn't!

1ST V.   She did!

VICAR.   We must.

3RD V.   Yes.

4TH V.   No.

VOICES [*in crescendo*].

     Good.

        Bad.

           Poor.

              Rich.

                 White.

                    Black.

                       High.

                           Low.

   Touch.

       Find.

          Pay.

             Eat.

               Weep.

                 Hurt.

                    Come.

                       Go.

   Boy.

       Tea.

          Lamb.

            Crewe.

                Shame.

                   Price.

                       O!

[*The hubbub is interrupted by the* VICAR, *who mounts on to a chair and begins ringing a Stationmaster's bell. Everybody is silent.*]

VICAR. Ladies and Gentlemen. I think that there
Are several strangers to Pressan here.
On your behalf I give them greeting
And will explain the purpose of our meeting:

The ancient family of Crewe
(It may perhaps be known to you)
For generations owned the land,
The farms, the fields on which we stand.
Sir Bingham Crewe, who was the last,
(God rest his soul, for he has passed)
We touched our hats to, had a son,
A handsome lad, his only one,
Called Francis, who was to succeed him.
Would he were here! We badly need him.
They quarrelled, I am sad to say,
And so, ten years ago today,
Young Francis packed and ran away
Leaving behind him no address.
Where he has gone, we cannot guess;
For since that day no news at all
Of where he is has reached the Hall.
In fact, we do not even know
If he be living still or no.

Sir Bingham died eight years ago,
Francis his heir being missing still,

And left these clauses in his will:
Each year, his villages in turn
Should choose by lottery a man
To find Sir Francis if he can :
Further, he promised half his land,
And Iris his daughter adds her hand
In marriage to the lucky one
Who comes home with his only son.

This year is Pressan's turn to choose.
Oh may this year bring the good news!

A VILLAGER [*sings*].

It seems such ages since the Master's son
   Went away.
He left his books, his clothes, his boots, his
   car, his gun
   On that dreadful summer's day.
He vanished suddenly without a single
   word of warning:
   Left us alone to make our moan;
   He left us mourning.

CHORUS.

Why has Fate been blind to our tears?
Why has she been so unkind to our fears?
Who shall we send this time who shall look
   for him,
Search every corner and cranny and nook
   for him?
   It may be you the lot will fall upon,
   It may be me the lot will call upon

23

                      To guide back
                      With pride back
                      Our young heir Sir Francis Crewe!
VILLAGER.   Without his face we don't know what to do,
                      We're undone.
                      He was a beauty with a sense of duty too,
                      He was our brother and our son.
                      His wit, his charm, his strength, his man-
                          ners, his modesty and his virtue
                      Were we to tell, your contrast, well,
                      With him would hurt you.
CHORUS.   Why has Fate . . . etc.
CURATE [*to the* VICAR]. The names have all come in.
                      We're ready to begin.
VICAR.   Excellent. Excellent.
                      [*A top hat is passed to him by the* POLICE
                      SERGEANT.]
                                                  Do you swear
                      That all the names are written here
                      Of every man in this village alive,
                      Unmarried and over twenty-five?
SERGEANT. I swear it.
VICAR.   Miss Iris Crewe.
                                      [IRIS *comes forward.*]
                      Iris Crewe, are you willing now
                      In the presence of these people to make
                          your vow?
IRIS.   I am.
VICAR [IRIS *repeats each phrase after him*].
                      I, Iris Crewe, do solemnly swear
                                   24

In the presence of these people here,
That I will be the wedded wife
To love and cherish all my life
Of him, whoever he may be,
Who brings my brother back to me.

VICAR.   Read the names of those we sent
Who failed to do the thing they meant.

SERGEANT. Nobby Sollers.
Sorbo Lamb.
Frenchie Joe.
Chimp Eagle.
The Midget.
Muffin Todd.
Nicky Peterson.

[*The* VICAR's *eyes are bound with a hand-kerchief. He stirs the hat and draws, saying:*]

Divvy Divvy Divvy Divvy Divvy DivvyDi
Divvy Divvy Divvy Divvy Divvy Divvy Di.
Swans in the air. Swans in the air.
Let the chosen one appear!

CURATE [*taking paper from him and reading*].
Alan Norman.

[*A short burst of cheering.*]

VICAR [*removing the bandage*]. Alan Norman.

[ALAN *comes forward and kneels.*]

Alan Norman, will you go
Cross any border in sand or snow,
Will you do whatever may be needful
Though people and customs both be hateful,
When mind and members go opposite way,

25

Watching wake folding long on sea;
Will you remain a passenger still
Nor desperate plunge for home?

ALAN.   I will.

VICAR [*producing a bag*]. Here is what the trustees give
That as you journey you may live:
Five hundred pounds; no more, no less.
May it help you to success.

[ALAN *accepts the bag and bows.*]

Let us stand a moment in silent prayer.

[*All the men present remove their hats. The*
DOG *enters and begins sniffing about. People*
surreptitiously kick it or pat it, but it re-
fuses to stay quiet.]

SEMI-CHORUS I.   Enter with him
These legends, love,
For him assume
Each diverse form
As legend simple
As legend queer
That he may do
What these require
Be, love, like him
To legend true.

SEMI-CHORUS II. When he to ease
His heart's disease
Must cross in sorrow
Corrosive seas
As dolphin go,
As cunning fox

26

Guide through the rocks,
Tell in his ear
The common phrase
Required to please
The guardians there.
And when across
The livid marsh
Big birds pursue
Again be true
Between his thighs
As pony rise
As swift as wind
Bear him away
Till cries and they
Are left behind.

CHORUS. But when at last
These dangers past
His grown desire
Of legends tire
O then, love, standing
At legends' ending,
Claim your reward
Submit your neck
To the ungrateful stroke
Of his reluctant sword
That starting back
His eyes may look
Amazed as you
Find what he wanted
Is faithful too

27

But disenchanted
Your simplest love.

VICAR.　Well, Alan, let me congratulate
You first and then ourselves and Fate.
We couldn't have chosen a better man.
If you can't succeed, then no one can.

[*Sees* DOG.]

There's that dog again! I'm blest!
I thought I'd lost him like the rest.
George, George! Good dog! Come here!
Walk George, walk.

[*He whistles. The* DOG *runs away.*]
That's queer!

[*Everyone looks at the* DOG, *who walks round, snuffling and refusing advances.*]

GENERAL. If you ask me, I shouldn't wonder if that dog wasn't sickening for the rabies. Most extraordinary animal I ever came across. Turns up on your doorstep one morning with his tongue hanging out, like the prodigal son; lets you feed him, slobber over him, pet him, makes himself quite at home. In an hour or two he's one of the family. And then, after a week or a fortnight, he'll be off again, cool as you please. Doesn't know you if you meet him in the street. And he's played the same trick on all of us. Confounded ungrateful brute! It's his mongrel blood, of course. No loyalty; no proper feeling. Though I'm bound to say, while he was with me he was the best gun-dog I ever had. [*To* DOG.] Come here, sir. Heel, sir. Heel!!

[*The Dog regards the General for a moment with an almost human contempt. Then it continues its snuffling.*]

VILLAGERS. Isn't he sweet?
Here is some meat.
If he were to choose
Me, I couldn't refuse.
If he'd come to me
I'd give him cake for tea.
[*The Dog reaches Alan and begins to fawn upon him and wag its tail.*]

VILLAGERS. Oh look! He's chosen you!
What are you going to do?

ALAN. I'll take him too.

ALL. You must name him anew.

ALAN. For luck I'll call him Francis.

ALL. Oh, look how he prances!

BUS CONDUCTOR. The village bus is about to start
Those who are coming prepare to depart.

VICAR [*giving a small parcel to Alan*].
Here is a tin of Church of England Mixture
Just to show you that our friendship is a fixture.
Smoke it while you are a vagrant
And may it keep our memory fragrant.

CURATE. I have a little present here,
It's just some trustworthy underwear.
May its high-grade Botany wool
Keep you warm and keep you cool.

29

VILLAGE CHEMIST.
          Here is some Victo for the nerves, in case
          The Man Next Door should take your place.
A SCOUTMASTER. Here is a Kron watch; like a wife
          To keep exact time all your life,
          Generously designed to offer beauty
          And like an Englishman to do its duty.
          A nameless watch is scarcely better
          Than an anonymous letter.
            [*During these speeches, the* GENERAL *has
            been having a whispered consultation with
            his* WIFE.]
GENERAL'S WIFE. Oh *no*, dear! I'm sure ten shillings
               would be *ample*.
GENERAL [*advancing pompously to* ALAN].
          Ahem! Ahem!
            [*He gives money with the air of tipping a
            porter.*]
             Don't disgrace Pressan Ambo, my boy.
ALAN.   Rather not, sir! Thanks awfully, sir!
IRIS.   Alan dearest, we must part
            But keep this photo near your heart,
            Wherever you go, by land or sea,
            Look on this and think of me:
            For whatever you must do
            My thoughts are always with you too.
ALAN.   Iris, give me a parting kiss
            In promise of our future bliss.
IRIS.   Gladly, Alan, I give you this.
                              [*Embrace.*]
                    30

VOICES.   Oh dear, its beginning to rain!
            You ought to weed it.
            The farmers need it.
            Mummy, I've got a pain.
ALL.   Speech! Speech!
ALAN.   You've been so ripping and kind
            It puts all words out of my mind,
            But if there's anything I can do,
            Ladies and Gentlemen, for you. . . .
MILDRED LUCE [*suddenly appearing*].   Yes!
            Set off for Germany and shoot them all!
            Poison the wells, till her people drink the
                sea
            And perish howling. Strew all her fields
            With arsenic, leave a land whose crops
            Would starve the unparticular hyena!
            But you are young and it is useless
            To look to Youth. In the November Silence
            I have heard more shuffling every year,
            Seen more of the up-to-date young men
                there Waiting
            Impatient in the crowd to catch a train
            And shake a German gently by the hand.
            I had two sons as tall as you :
            A German sniper shot them both.
            They crawled to me across the floor ;
            I put their earliest prattle in a book.
            A German sniper shot them both.
            I saw them win prizes at their prep-school
                sports;

31

I had their friends at half-term out to tea.
A German sniper shot them both.
I heard their voices alter as they grew
Shyer of me and more like men.
                                   [*Taking out a large watch.*]
O Ticker, Ticker, they are dead
As the Grimaldi infants.
Justice has gone a summer cruise and let
Her mansion to a madman. Say something
Ticker. Nothing. Nothing. I protest.

VICAR.   Mildred dear, go home and rest
And calm yourself. That will be best.
                                   [*Sounds of a motor-horn.*]

BUS-CONDUCTOR. The bus is leaving in a minute:
Those who are coming must step in it.

ALAN AND CHORUS. Now {I / we} must part

It's time to start

With tears in {my / our} eyes {I / we} say goodbyes.

Success be with you and satisfaction
We wish to you in your every action.
In July and December

{I / we} will remember you!

   [ALAN *goes out.* ALL *wave handkerchiefs
   and hands.*]

CURTAIN

CHORUS

Salmon leaping the ladder, eel in damp grass, the mole
    and the tiercel:
Such images of travel do not apply.
Our impulses are unseasonal and image-ridden: our trif-
    ling disturbances are without crisis.
Our sex and our sorrow are ever about us, like the sultri-
    ness of a summer
As about our hero on his human journey,
Crossing a channel: on sea in steamer
For Ostnia and Westland, in post-war Europe.

    Creatures of air and darkness, from this hour
        Put and keep our friend in power.
    Let not the reckless heavenly riders
        Treat him and us as rank outsiders.

    From the accosting sickness and
        Love's fascinating biassed hand,
    The lovely grievance and the false address,
        From con-man and coiner protect and bless.

SCENE II

[*The saloon of a Channel steamer. Behind the bar, the* BARMAN *is polishing glasses. The two* JOURNALISTS *are seated, drinking. A small piano against the wall.*]

1ST JOURNALIST. The Old Man sent for me before I left. Wants me to get the low-down on the Dripping Merger. Officially, I'm covering the Danube floods.

2ND J. I saw Timmy last night. He's just back from the Carpathians. Tight as usual. He had all the dope about the Army Contracts trial. Some kid, Timmy.

1ST J. I heard a bit about that from Gus. Blankets, wasn't it?

2ND J. Blankets nothing! Why, man, it was tarpaulin!

1ST J. You've got it wrong, old horse. Gus said five million blankets.

2ND J. Six million. . . .

1ST J. Gus swears it was five.

2ND J. To Hell with Gus. As I was saying, these tarpaulins. . . .

1ST J. My dear old fish, Gus had it from the War Minister himself. . . . 'Blankets', he said. . . .

34

2ND J. Boy, you give me a pain. The whole *beauty* of the thing was that they were tarpaulins, don't you see . . . ?

> [*Enter* ALAN *and the* DOG. *The* JOURNALISTS *stop arguing and watch him.* ALAN *crosses the stage to the bar.*]

ALAN [*diffidently*]. A double whisky, please: And a glass of milk.

BARMAN. Certainly, sir.

ALAN [*embarrassed*]. And I wonder if you'd mind putting the whisky in a bowl?

BARMAN [*puzzled*]. A bowl, sir?

ALAN. It's for my dog, you see.

> [*The* BARMAN *winks at the* JOURNALISTS. 1ST JOURNALIST *taps his head significantly.* 2ND JOURNALIST *nods agreement.*]

BARMAN [*suavely*]. Ah, to be sure, sir.

ALAN [*confidentially*]. Did *you* ever hear of a dog drinking whisky before? *I* never did. I only found it out as we were coming down on the train. An old gent in our compartment had ordered a bottle, and, before you could say Jack Robinson, Francis had swallowed the lot!

BARMAN. Most remarkable, sir. Water or soda, sir?

> [*The* DOG *begins howling.*]

ALAN. Rather not! He always drinks it neat, don't you, Francis, old boy? [*The* DOG *wags its tail.*] Perhaps we'd better say two double whiskies. It doesn't look much when you pour it into a bowl, does it? [*The* BARMAN *adds the whiskies.* ALAN *gives the bowl to*

35

the DOG, *who laps eagerly*.] You see? And he won't touch anything else. I've tried him with tea, coffee, cocoa, lemonade, beer, wine, everything you can thing of . . . I'm afraid I'm going to find it rather expensive.

[*He sighs and sips his glass of milk.*]

BARMAN. You're teetotal yourself, I see, sir?

ALAN [*blushing*]. Ha ha! You mustn't think I've given it up on moral grounds, or any rot of that sort. . . . The fact is, I only started yesterday. You see, I want to keep a clear head all the time. I've got some rather difficult business to settle.

BARMAN. Indeed, sir?

ALAN. Yes. I'm looking for someone. Perhaps you might be able to help me? Have you been working on this boat for long?

BARMAN. A matter of fifteen years, sir.

ALAN. Why, that's splendid! Then you're almost sure to have seen him. His name's Francis Crewe.

BARMAN. Can't say that I seem to recall it, sir. Can you describe him at all?

ALAN. Well, no. I'm afraid I can't do that. You see, he left home ten years ago and that was before we came to live in the village. Here's the only photograph they'd got of him. It isn't much use. It was taken when he was six months old.

BARMAN [*examining photo*]. Bless his little heart! Why, he's the spit and image of what my Jacky used to be. And now he can lift his poor old father up with one arm. In the marines, is my Jacky. Getting married next month.

36

ALAN. I'm getting married too, soon. At least, I hope I am. Look, here's a picture of my fiancee. What do you think of her? Isn't she a ripper?

BARMAN. I congratulate you, sir.

[*The* DOG *growls.*]

ALAN. Shut up, Francis, you old silly! [*To* BARMAN.] It's an extraordinary thing: Whenever I show that photograph of Iris to anybody, he begins to growl. Just as though he were jealous. . . . Here, Francis. Shake a paw.

[*The* DOG *turns away.*]

BARMAN. You see, sir, he's offended. [*Slily.*] If you were to offer him another whisky, he'd be ready to make it up, I'm sure.

ALAN [*reluctantly*]. All right, if you think so.

[*The* DOG *immediately turns round and begins barking and licking* ALAN's *hand.*]

BARMAN. What did I tell you, sir? Nobody can resist a good whisky.

[*He looks pointedly at the bottle.*]

ALAN. I say, I'm most awfully sorry. I ought to have asked you if you'd have a drink, too.

BARMAN. Well, sir: Since you're so pressing.

ALAN. By the way, have you ever been to Ostnia?

BARMAN. Can't say I have, sir. My brother was waiter at the Grand Hotel in the capital at one time.

ALAN. Do you know if it's the sort of country where people are likely to get lost?

BARMAN. I'm not sure I take your meaning, sir.

37

ALAN. You see, I thought of beginning my search there. I didn't know where to start, so I just shut my eyes and put my finger on the map.

BARMAN. And a very good idea too, sir. Your health, sir. [*They touch glasses. The* DOG *lifts up the bowl in its paws and touches* ALAN'S *glass. They all drink.*]

1ST J. What do you make of him?

2ND J. Queer sort of card. Might be a munitions agent.

1ST J. Doubt it. I know most of them by sight.

2ND J. Or in the dope traffic.

1ST J. Hasn't got a scarab ring.

2ND J. A white slaver?

1ST J. They generally wear spats.

2ND J. Secret Service, maybe.

1ST J. With that tie? Not on your life!

2ND J. There's something phoney about him, anyhow. Come on, let's get acquainted. There'll be a story in it, you bet. [*Loudly, to* ALAN.] Pardon me, sir. Did I hear you saying just now that you were travelling to Ostnia?

ALAN. Why, yes. Can you tell me anything about it? I'd be ever so grateful.

1ST J. Can we? I should say so! My colleague here knows Ostnia like the inside of his hat.

2ND J. Pretty little country, Ostnia. Biggest national debt and lowest birth-rate in Europe. Half the budget goes into frontier forts, which are no more use than a headache because the contractor's a crook. The railways are so old they aren't safe, the mines

38

are mostly flooded and the factories do nothing but catch fire. The Commander-in-Chief is no better than a bandit: He makes all the big stores pay for protection. The Archbishop spends his time copying naval plans for the Westland Intelligence Bureau. And meanwhile, the peasants die of typhus. Believe me, kid, it's God's own land.

ALAN. I say! It must be awfully dangerous there, isn't it?

1ST J. Not for tourists. They only see the mountains and the Renaissance Palace. . . . Of course, when you get behind the scenes, you're liable to be bumped off if you don't watch out.

ALAN. I shall have to be careful, then. You see, I'm looking for someone named Francis Crewe. . . .

2ND J. See here, boy. You can keep that blue-eyed stuff for the others. You don't have to do it on us. We're not inquisitive.

1ST J. Don't worry. We'll show you the ropes.

2ND J. Maybe we should introduce ourselves. I'm on the *Thunderbolt.*

1ST J. And I'm the live wire of the *Evening Moon.*

ALAN [*shaking hands*]. I say! Are you really? I've always wanted to meet some proper writers. [*To* DOG.] Francis, come here and be introduced!

> [*The* DOG *leaves the bar and comes over to them. It is obviously intoxicated. It makes the* JOURNALISTS *a profound bow.*]

1ST J. That's a pretty cute hound of yours. What'll you take for him?

39

ALAN. Oh, I couldn't posssibly sell him, thank you. Why, I wouldn't be parted from Francis for a thousand pounds. You've no idea how clever he is. It's quite uncanny, sometimes. . . . Francis, show the gentlemen what you can do.

> [*The* DOG *attempts to balance a chair on his nose, but is too drunk to do so. Suddenly he rushes out of the saloon and is seen leaning over the rail of the ship.*]

2ND J. Your canine friend appears to be slightly overcome.

ALAN. Poor Francis! He'll be better soon. I hope it'll be a lesson to him. . . . Do please go on with what you were telling me. It's so awfully interesting. Tell me about some other countries.

2ND J. All countries are the same. Everywhere you go, it's the same: Nothing but a racket!

> [*The* 1ST JOURNALIST *goes to the piano and begins to play.*]

2ND J. [*singing*]. The General Public has no notion
> Of what's behind the scenes.
> They vote at times with some emotion
> But don't know what it means.
> Doctored information
> Is all they have to judge things by;
> The hidden situation
> Develops secretly.

CHORUS. If the Queen of Poland swears,
> If the Pope kicks his cardinals down the stairs,

If the Brazilian Consul
   Misses his train at Crewe,
   If Irish Clergy
   Loose their energy
   And dons have too much to do:
The reason is just simply this:
   They're in the racket, too.

1ST J.   To grasp the morning dailies you must
   Read between the lines.
The evening specials make just nonsense
   Unless you've shares in mines.
National estrangements
Are not what they seem to be;
   Underground arrangements
Are the master-key.

CHORUS. If Chanel gowns have a train this year,
   If Morris cars fit a self-changing gear,
   If Lord Peter Whimsey
   Misses an obvious clue,
   If Wallace Beery
   Should act a fairy
   And Chaplin the Wandering Jew;
The reason is
Just simply this:
   They're in the racket, too!

[*The* DOG *re-enters the Saloon. He holds out his arms to* ALAN. *They dance. The* BARMAN *juggles with the cocktail-shaker*.]

2ND J.   There's lots of little things that happen
   Almost every day

That show the way the wind is blowing
    So keep awake, we say.
We have got the lowdown
    On all European affairs;
To History we'll go down
    As the men with the longest ears.
CHORUS. If the postman is three minutes late,
    If the grocer's boy scratches your gate,
If you get the wrong number,
    If Cook has burnt the stew,
If all your rock-plants
Come up as dock-plants
    And your tennis-court turns blue;
The reason is just simply this:
    You're in the racket, too!

CURTAIN

CHORUS

                     Ostnia and Westland;
Products of the peace which that old man provided,
Of the sobriquet of Tiger senilely vain.
Do not content yourself with their identification,
Saying: This is the southern country with the shape of
      Cornwall,
Or the Danube receives the effluence from this: Or that
      must shiver in the Carpathian shadow.
Do not comfort yourself with the reflection: 'How very
      unEnglish'
If your follies are different, it is because you are richer;
Your clocks have completed fewer revolutions since the
      complacent years
When Corelli was the keeper of the Avon Swan
And the naughty life-forcer in the norfolk jacket
Was the rebels' only uncle.
                Remember more clearly their suaver images:
The glamour of the cadet-schools, the footmen and the
      enormous hats.
But already, like an air-bubble under a microscope-
      slide, the film of poverty is expanding
And soon it will reach your treasure and your gentle-
      manly behaviour.
Observe, therefore, and be more prepared than our hero.

SCENE III

[*Ostnia. Before the Palace. A* POLICEMAN *on duty.*
Enter ALAN, *the* JOURNALISTS *and the* DOG.]

1ST J.   The trams are stopped, the streets are still,

    Black flags hang from each window-sill

    And the whole city is in mourning.

    The King can't have died?

2ND J.   We had no warning.

1ST J.   You ask the bobby on the corner there.

2ND J. Officer, what's happening here?

POLICEMAN. Twelfth of the month, sir: Execution Day

    There's been a revolt, I'm sorry to say.

2ND J. Another?

    But you had one when I was here before.

POLICEMAN. When was that, sir?

2ND J.   Only last May.

POLICEMAN. Since then, we've had four.

    We have them every fortnight, now;

    But they're generally over without much row.

    We round them up and then the King

    Himself arranges everything.   [*Salutes.*]

    Go inside and see. Strangers are always in-
    vited.

    I know His Majesty will be delighted.

44

1st J.   Boy, what a scoop!
             I'm cock a whoop!
               Have you got your pencil?
             It's quite essential.
[*The* JOURNALISTS *go into the Palace, followed
by* ALAN *and the* DOG.]

CURTAIN

45

SCENE IV

[*Ostnia. A room in the Palace.* KING, QUEEN, COUR-
TIERS, PRIESTS. *An organ voluntary is just finishing.*
The MASTER OF THE CEREMONIES *approaches the*
KING.]

M.C. Everything is ready, your Majesty.

KING. You've had a dress rehearsal, I hope? We don't
want any hitches this time.

M.C. Yes, your Majesty. I took your part myself. With
a dummy revolver, of course.

KING. And what about my little suggestion?

M.C. We've cut the Dies Irae, your Majesty.

KING. Good. I'm so glad you agree with me. I heard
several complaints last time, that it was too grue-
some. As you know, I am particularly anxious not
to hurt anybody's feelings. It's a beautiful piece, of
course, but one can't expect them to be quite edu-
cated up to it yet. One has to make allowances. . . .
Oh, and by the way, you might tell the male alto to
moderate his top notes a bit. Last time, he gave the
Queen a headache.

M.C. I will, your Majesty.

46

KING. Excellent. Then I think we can begin. Bring in the prisoners. [*To the* QUEEN.] My dear, your crown is a little crooked. Allow me.

> [*Solemn music.* The PRISONERS, *with their wives and mothers, are brought in. The* PRISONERS *are workmen, dressed neatly in their Sunday clothes. The women, like the ladies of the court, are dressed in black.*]

CHOIR. Requiem aeternam dona et lux perpetua luceat eis.

KING [*rising to address the* PRISONERS]. Gentlemen. I do not intend to keep you long; but I cannot let this opportunity slip by without saying how much I and the Queen appreciate and admire the spirit in which you have acted and how extremely sorry we both are that our little differences can only be settled in this er . . . somewhat drastic fashion.

Believe me, I sympathise with your aims from the bottom of my heart. Are we not all socialists nowadays? But as men of the world I am sure you will agree with me that order has to be maintained. In spite of everything which has happened, I do want us to keep this solemn moment free from any thought of malice. If any of you have a complaint to make about your treatment, I hope you will say so now before it is too late. You haven't? I am very glad indeed to hear it. Before going on to the next part of the ceremony, let me conclude by wishing you Bon Voyage and every happiness in the next world.

[*Music. The* PRISONERS *are led out. A foot-
man brings a gold revolver on a cushion and pre-
sents it to the* KING, *who follows the* PRI-
SONERS.]

CANTOR. Kyrie eleison.

CHOIR. Mars eleison.

CANTOR. Kyrie eleison.

CANTOR. Homo natus de muliere, brevi vivens tempore,
repletur multis miseriis. Qui quasi flos egreditur et
conteritur et fugit velut umbra, et nunquam in
eodem statu permanet.

Media via in morte sumus: quem quaerimus ad-
jutorem nisi te, Domine, qui pro peccatis nostris
juste irasceris?

Sancte Zeus, sancto fortis, sancte et misericors
Salvator amaris mortis aeternae poenis ne tradas
nos. Mars omnipotens. Frater Jovis, qui tollis pec-
cata mundi.

CHOIR. Miserere nobis.

CANTOR. Qui tollis peccata mundi.

CHOIR. Miserere nobis.

CANTOR. Qui tollis peccata mundi.

CHOIR. Suscipe deprecationem nostram.

CANTOR. Qui sedet ad dextram Jovis.

CHOIR. Miserere nobis.

[*Shots are heard, off. The Last Post is sounded.*]

CHOIR. Proficiscere Anima Ostniana, de hoc mundo.

[*Re-enter the* KING. *A footman brings a silk
handkerchief to clean the revolver. Another foot-
man brings a basin of water and a towel. The*

48

KING *washes his hands. The four corpses are brought in on stretchers.*]

CHOIR. Rex tremendae majestatis, qui salvandos salvas gratis salva me fons pietatis.

[*Trumpet.*]

M.C. Her Majesty the Queen will now address the bereaved.

QUEEN [*to the wives and mothers of the* PRISONERS]. Ladies (or may I call you Sisters?) On this day of national sorrow, my woman's heart bleeds for you. I too am a mother. I too have borne the pangs of childbirth and known the unutterable comfort of seeing a little curly head asleep on my breast. I too am a wife and have lain in the strong arms of the beloved. Remember, then, in your loss, that in all you suffer, I suffer with you. And remember that Suffering is Woman's fate and Woman's glory. By suffering we are ennobled; we rise to higher things. Be comforted, therefore, and abide patiently, strong in the hope that you will meet your loved ones again in another and better world where there are no tears, no pains, no misunderstandings; where we shall all walk hand in hand from everlasting to everlasting.

M.C. The ladies of the Court will offer the bereaved some light refreshment.

[*The* LADIES *take round champagne and cakes to the* PRISONERS' WOMEN.]

A WOMAN [*with a sudden hysterical scream*]. Murderers!!

[*All the* WOMEN *are instantly and politely re-*

49

moved by footmen. The Courtiers *cough and look at the ceiling in pained embarrassment.*]

King. Poor things! They don't really mean it, you know.

Queen. They lead such terrible lives!

[*All the* Courtiers *sigh deeply. The* Ladies *of the court begin to admire the corpses.*]

1st Lady. How lovely they look:

Like pictures in a children's book!

2nd L. Look at this one. He seems so calm,

As if he were asleep with his head in his arm.

He's the handsomest, don't you think, of the four?

How I wish I'd met him before!

I'll put some blood on my hanky, a weeny spot,

So that he never shall be forgot.

3rd L. Oh Duchess, isn't he just a duck!

His fiancee certainly had the luck.

He can't have been more than nineteen, I should say.

He must have been full of Vitamin A.

2nd L. Dear Lady Emily,

What a clever simile!

4th L. What beautiful hair; as white as wool!

And such strong hands. Why, they're not yet cool!

Lend me a pair of scissors, dear.

I want a lock as a souvenir.

M.C. Three Englishmen crave an audience with your Majesty.

KING. Oh, certainly, certainly. I'll see them at once.

[*Trumpet.*]

M.C. Mr Alan Norman and friends.

[*Enter* ALAN *and the two* JOURNALISTS. *They kiss the* KING's *hand.*]

KING. How do you do? Delighted to see anyone from England. I have very happy memories of visits there before the War. The singing in King's Chapel was marvellous, quite marvellous. And Melba, ah, delicious! Talking of which, I hope you liked our singing today? I'm always most grateful for any criticisms. . . . How's London? My dear London! Those evenings at the Crystal Palace! What a building! What fireworks! I hear Regent Street is quite unrecognizable now. Dear me, how time flies, hm, indeed, yes. . . . But I mustn't bore you with an old man's memories. What can I do for you?

ALAN. I'm looking for Sir Francis Crewe:

Is his name, Sire, known to you?

KING. Sir Francis Crewe? Hm, let me think. He wasn't one of your ambassadors, by any chance? I'm so stupid about names. [*To the* MASTER OF CERE-MONIES.] Ask the Court if they know anything about an Englishman called Sir Francis Crewe.

[*Trumpet.*]

M.C. Is an Englishman, Sir Francis Crewe,

Familiar to anyone of you?

[*Silence.*]

KING. You see? I'm so sorry. . . . But I tell you what: You might try the Red Light District. It's always

51

full of foreign visitors. [*To* M.C.] Is the Crown Prince in?

M.C. No, your Majesty.

KING. What a pity. He'd have been delighted to show you round. He's always going down there. It worries the Queen dreadfully, but I tell her not to take it to heart so: Boys will be boys. . . . Have you got a plan of the city?

M.C. Here's one, your Majesty.

KING. Thanks. [*Opening the plan, to* ALAN.] Come round on this side, you'll see better. Here's the Palace and here's the Palace Underground Station, just opposite. You take the tube to the Triangle: It's a two angel fare, I think. Then you take a number four tram to the Butter Kiln. After that, I'm afraid you'll have to walk. Keep left at the Cemetery.

M.C. Excuse me, your Majesty, but the trams aren't running and everything's shut because of the executions.

KING. Of course! How silly of me to forget! Ring up the Broadcasting Station at once and have the mourning called off.

[M.C. *bows and retires.*]

KING. Well, goodbye, and I hope you find your friend. I'm sorry we couldn't do more for you. . . . By the by, are you sure you didn't see anything in the least bit out of taste in our ceremony? I always think the English have such good taste in matters of ritual. You didn't? that's very encouraging.

When you get back to England, remember me to Lord Harborne, if he's still alive. One of the real old English eccentrics. Used to breakfast at midnight on champagne and raw beef. . . . Won't you have a drink before you go?

ALAN. No thank you, your Majesty. You see, we haven't got much time.

KING. Well, goodbye. Goodbye. [*Aside to the* M.C. *crossly.*] What on earth is the band-master thinking of? Tell him to play something suitable at once, in honour of our guests.

 [*As* ALAN *and the* JOURNALISTS *retire backwards, bowing; the band begins to play* 'Rule, Britannia'.]

CURTAIN

CHORUS

You with shooting-sticks and cases for field-glasses,
  your limousines parked in a circle: who visit the
  public games, observing in burberries the feats of
  the body:
You who stand before the west fronts of cathedrals: ap-
  praising the curious carving:
The virgin creeping like a cat to the desert, the trumpet-
  ting angels, the usurers boiling:
And you also who look for truth: alone in tower:
Follow our hero and his escort on his latest journey:
  From the square surrounded by Georgian houses,
  take the lurching tram eastward
South of the ship-cranes, of the Slythe canal: Stopping
  at Fruby and Drulger Street,
Past boys ball-using: shrill in alleys.
Passing the cinemas blazing with bulbs: bowers of
  bliss
Where thousands are holding hands: they gape at the
  tropical vegetation, at the Ionic pillars and the
  organ solo.
Look left: The moon shows locked sheds, wharves by
  water,

On your right is the Power House: its chimneys fume
   gently above us like rifles recently fired.
Look through the grating at the vast machinery: at the
   dynamos and turbines
Grave, giving no sign of the hurricane of steam within
   their huge steel bottles,
At the Diesel engines like howdahed elephants: at the
   dials with their flickering pointers:
Power to the city: where loyalties are not those of the
   family.

And now, enter:
O human pity, gripped by the crying of a captured bird
   wincing at sight of surgeon's lance,
Shudder indeed: that life on its narrow littoral so lucky
Can match against eternity a time so cruel!
The street we enter with setts is paved: cracked and un-
   even as an Alpine glacier,
Garbage chucked in the gutters has collected in the hol-
   lows in loathsome pools,
Back to back houses on both sides stretch: a dead-
   straight line of dung-coloured brick
Wretched and dirty as a run for chickens.
Full as a theatre is the foul throughfare: some sitting
   like sacks, some slackly standing,
Their faces grey in the glimmering gaslight: their eye-
   balls drugged like a dead rabbit's,
From a window a child is looking, by want so fretted his
   face has assumed the features of a tortoise:
A human forest: all by one infection cancelled.

Despair so far invading every tissue has destroyed in
these the hidden seat of the desire and the intelli-
gence.

A little further, and now: Enter the street of some of
your dreams:
Here come the untidy jokers and the spruce who love
military secrets
And those whose houses are dustless and full of Ming
vases:
Those rebels who have freed nothing in the whole uni-
verse from the tyranny of the mothers, except a
tiny sensitive area:
Those who are ashamed of their baldness or the size of
their members,
Those suffering from self deceptions necessary to life
And all who have compounded envy and hopelessness
into desire
Perform here nightly their magical acts of identification
Among the Chinese lanterns and the champagne served
in shoes.
You may kiss what you like; it has often been kissed be-
fore.
Use what words you wish; they will often be heard again.

SCENE V

[*Ostnia. A street in the Red Light District. Each café has a small lighted peep-hole, resembling a theatre box-office. Above each of the four peep-holes is a sign-board with the name:* TIGER JACK'S. YAMA THE PIT. COSY CORNER. MOTHER HUBBARD'S. *The heads of the four proprietors are visible at the peep-holes.*]

FOUR PROPRIETORS [*singing together*].

> To Red Lamp Street you are all invited;
> Here Plato's halves are at last united.
> Whatever you dream of alone in bed,
> Come to us and we will make it real instead.

TIGER JACK. Do you feel like a bit of fun?

> At Tiger Jack's you will find it done.
> We've girls of eighty and women of four;
> Let them teach you things you never knew before.

PROPRIETRESS OF YAMA THE PIT.

> Or does the thought of a thorough whipping
> By ladies in boots set your pulses skipping.
> At Yama the Pit you must pay a call
> And soon you won't be able to sit down at all.

BOSS OF COSY CORNER.

> But perhaps you're a woman-scorner?

Then step inside at the Cosy Corner.
We've boys of every shape and size:
Come and gaze into their great big eyes.

MOTHER HUBBARD. If you've taken a fancy to snow,
Mother Hubbard's the place to go.
With Cokey Minnie and Dopey Jim
You can hold a party till the stars are dim.

ALL TOGETHER. Ladies and gentlemen, bear in mind
Kisses in the graveyard are hard to find.
'Tempus fugit', the poet said:
So come to us at once for you will soon be dead.

> [*Enter* ALAN, *the* JOURNALISTS *and the* DOG.
> *They are immediately accosted by two touts. The*
> 1ST TOUT *is very old and bleary. The* 2ND
> TOUT *is a boy of eight.*]

1ST T. Buy a post-card, guvnor?

2ND T. Come wiv me. Good Jig-a-Jig.

ALAN [*going up to* TIGER JACK].
Good evening. Is Sir Francis Crewe,
English, known perhaps to you?

TIGER JACK. Money, money
Makes our speech as sweet as honey.

> [ALAN *gives money.*]

Now ask again
And not in vain.

ALAN. Good evening. Is Sir Francis Crewe,
English, known perhaps to you?

TIGER JACK. Phyllis, Lou,
All of you,
Have you heard of Sir Francis Crewe?

58

VOICES [*from within*]. A Francis I knew
        (a nice boy, too)
        And I a Crewe.
        But none of us know Sir Francis Crewe.
TIGER JACK. But stay.
        Here it is gay.
ALAN. No thank you, no.
        I must go.

                            [*Moves on.*]

1ST TOUT. Buy a post-card, guvnor?
2ND T. Come wiv me. Good Jig-a-Jig.
ALAN [*to* PROPRIETRESS OF YAMA THE PIT].
        Good evening. Is Sir Francis Crewe,
        English, known perhaps to you?
PROPRIETRESS OF Y.P. Money, money
        Makes our speech as sweet as honey.

                            [ALAN *gives money.*]

        You must pay more.

                            [ALAN *gives more.*]

        Now speak again,
        Not in vain.
ALAN. Good evening. Is Sir Francis Crewe,
        English, known perhaps to you?
PROPRIETRESS OF Y.P. Sue, Sue,
        That will do!
        He's already black and blue.
        Have you heard of Sir Francis Crewe?
SUE'S VOICE. I had an Englishman last year
        Who wore a pendant in each ear,
        Then there was one with a false nose:

It wasn't either of them, I suppose?
But stay,
Here it is gay.

ALAN. No thank you, no.
I must go.

[*Moves away.*]

1ST T. Buy a post-card, guvnor?

[2ND J. *buys one.*]

1ST J. [*looking at it over his shoulder, in disgust*].
Horrible hips and too much flesh:
Why can't they get hold of someone fresh?

2ND T. Come wiv me. Good Jig-a-Jig.

ALAN [*giving money to the* BOSS OF COSY CORNER].
Good Evening. Is Sir Francis Crewe,
English, known perhaps to you?

BOSS OF C.C.
You speak English? But I too!
Am I acquaint with Sir Francis Crewe?
Every English Lord come here.
Is it he in the corner there?
Wait a moment while I send
For Willy. . . . Willy,
How calls himself your English friend?

WILLY'S VOICE.
Harold. . . . Have you a cigarette for me?

BOSS OF C.C. Is it he?
Well, come inside and wait and see.
Many come in after ten.
Perhaps he will be one of them.

60

ALAN. No thank you, no.
I must go.

[*Moves away.*]

1ST J. Remember the sign.

2ND T. Come wiv me. Good Jig-a-Jig.

[1ST J. *chases him away.*]

2ND J. And say the line.

[ALAN *knocks three times at the door of* MOTHER HUBBARD'S.]

MOTHER HUBBARD. The cupboard was bare.

ALAN. And yet the poor dog got some.

[*Gives money.*]

Is the name Sir Francis Crewe,
English, known perhaps to you?

MOTHER HUBBARD.
Wait a moment, please. I'll get Dopey Jim.

[*She disappears.*]

1ST JOURNALIST. Hurry, hurry, do!
Our train leaves for Westland at twenty to.

2ND J. Chuck up hunting for your boy friend.
It's clear that he's come to a sticky end.

[*The face of a drug addict, hopelessly dazed, appears at the peep-hole.*]

ALAN. Good evening. Are you Mr Dopey Jim?

ADDICT. That's what they call me here: Up there, in the world, I had another name. For I could dance lightly and spring high like a rubber ball in the air: being champion at Flash Green of all such sports.

ALAN. You know Flash Green? Why, that's where Sorbo Lamb came from! He went away seven years

61

ago to look for Sir Francis Crewe. Did you ever meet him?

ADDICT. My mother bore no twins.

ALAN. Sorbo!

ADDICT. Alas.

ALAN. Oh, I am so glad! Whatever are you doing here? Have you seen Francis? Come along, we'll look for him together.

ADDICT. I may not leave this place.

ALAN. Do you mean they won't let you out? We'll soon see about that! There's four of us, and my dog can fight like a tiger. Just let them try to stop you!

ADDICT. You do not understand. [*Holds up his hands, which are free.*] Don't you see these chains? My punishment and my reward. The light of your world would dazzle me and its noises offend my ears. Fools! How could you possibly appreciate my exquisite pleasures? Sometimes I lie quite still for days together, contemplating the flame of a candle or the oscillating shadow of a lamp. What revelations, what bottomless despairs! Please leave me alone.

ALAN. Sorbo. . . . Isn't there anything I can do?

ADDICT. Yes. Tell them at Flash Green that I am dead. More I ask not. Farewell.

[*He disappears.*]

ALAN. What shall I do? What shall I do?
      I cannot find Sir Francis Crewe!

2ND J. Pull your socks up, kid, and don't make a fuss!
      Come along to Westland now with us.

Your friend may be there: You never know:
And we'll show you all there is to show.

[*All three exeunt with* Dog, *singing.*]

If yer wants to see me agyne
   Then come to the stytion before the tryne.
In the general wytin' 'all
   We'll see each other fer the very las' time of
      all!

[*The* Four Proprietors *sing, accompanied
by* First Tout *on the concertina and* Second
Tout *on the penny whistle.*]

All together.

Let us remember in a little song
Those who were with us but not for long.
Some were beautiful and some were gay
But Death's Black Maria took them all away.

Tiger Jack.

Lucky Lil got a rope of pearls,
Olive had autographed letters from earls,
Grace looked lovely when she danced the Fern
But Death took them yachting and they won't
   return.

Yama the Pit.

Pixie had a baron as a customer,
He bought a zeppelin, just for her.
You should have seen her with a hunting crop,
But in Death's sound-proof room she's got to
   stop.

Cosy Corner.

Tony the Kid looked a god in shorts,

Phil was asked to Switzerland for winter sports,
Jimmy sent them crazy in his thick white socks,
But Death has shut them all up in a long black
    box.

MOTHER HUBBARD.

Sammy and Di beat the gong around,
Wherever they walked there was snow on the
    ground.
Jessie and Colin had rings round their eyes
But Death put them where they can't get sup-
    plies.

ALL TOGETHER.

When we are dead we shan't thank for flowers,
We shan't hear the parson preaching for hours,
We shan't be sorry to be white bare bone
At last we shan't be hungry and can sleep alone.

CURTAIN

ACT II

SCENE I

[*Westland. A room in a lunatic asylum. At the back of the stage is a large portrait of a man in uniform: beneath which is written 'Our Leader'. The man has a loud-speaker instead of a face. The room is full of lunatics, male and female, who sit on their beds absorbed in various occupations or wander up and down the stage. On meeting each other, they exchange the Westland Salute: bringing the palm of the right hand smartly against the nape of the neck. Their manner is furtive and scared.*]

1st MAD LADY [*wanders across the stage, singing*].

> Seen when night was silent,
> The bean-shaped island
> And our ugly comic servant
> Who is observant.
> O the verandah and the fruit
> The tiny steamer in the bay
> Startling summer with its hoot.
> You have gone away.

1st LUNATIC [*whispering with* 2ND LUNATIC *in a corner*]. Heard any rumours?

2ND L. Heaps!

1st L. Oh, do tell me!

2ND L. Ssh! not so loud. I think they may be watching
us.

1ST L. I tell you what: I've got a plan. We'll say good-
bye now and then meet later, as if by accident.

2ND L. All right. But do be careful.

> [*They exchange the Westland Salute and separate
> to their respective beds.*]

> [*Enter* TWO MEDICAL OFFICERS *with* ALAN
> *in a strait-waistcoat, in a wheeled chair.*]

1ST M.O. The Ostnia Frontier wasn't it? They've sent us
several beauties.

2ND M.O. Yes.

1ST M.O. What do they say?

2ND M.O. Travelling with a dog.

1ST M.O. Hm. Canophilia.

1ST M.O. States he is looking for someone he doesn't
know.

2ND M.O. Phantasy Building. Go on.

1ST M.O. Doesn't know the Westland Song.

2ND M.O. Amnesia. Pretty serious. [*To* ALAN.] Now
you. Have you ever been to the North Pole?

ALAN. No.

1ST M.O. Can you speak Chinese?

ALAN. No!

2ND M.O. Do you dye your hair?

ALAN. No!

1ST M.O. Was your mother a negress?

ALAN. No!!

2ND M.O. Do you drink your bathwater?

ALAN. No!!!

1st M.O. Do you like my face ?

Alan [*losing his temper and yelling*]. No!!!!

1st M.O. Just as I feared, A typical case of negativism.

Alan. What are you going to do? Let me out of here.

2nd M.O. The gag, I think, don't you?

1st M.O. Yes, I think so.

[*They gag* Alan.]

2nd M.O. Quite classic. He'll be an ornament to our collection.

[*Exeunt* Medical Officers.]

2nd Mad Lady [*promenading with* 3rd M.L.]. The Leader says that next year he's going to put all us women into coops, like hens. And if we don't lay properly we shall be fattened for the Christmas Market.

3rd M.L. Oh, what a lovely idea!

2nd M.L. Yes, isn't it? And so beautiful, too. I mean, it will really make Motherhood sacred. And do away with all this horrible unwomanly nonsense about girls being independent. I'm sure *I* never wanted to be independent!

3rd M.L. I should think not, indeed! [*Shivers.*] Ugh, the idea!

[*Several* Lunatics *surround a* Lunatic *who is naked except for a bath-towel round his waist and has covered his body with smears of ink.*]

Naked Lunatic. I am the President of the newly-formed League of the Forefathers of Westland, which the Leader himself has officially approved. After careful historical investigations, I have discovered that this is the exact costume worn by the inhabitants of Westland two thousand years ago. All modern dress is effeminate and foreign. The L.F.W. will lead Westland back to the manly customs of our ancestors. Down with Machinery! Down with knives and forks! Down with bathrooms and books! Let us take to the woods and live on roots!

> [*The other* LUNATICS, *in great excitement, begin tearing off their clothes and scratching on the floor, as if to dig up plants from the ground. Meanwhile, the* 1ST *and* 2ND LUNATICS *leave their beds and greet each other with much ceremony.*]

1ST L. Ah, good morning, my dear Baron!

2ND L. Your Worship, this is indeed a pleasure!

1ST L. Remarkably mild weather, is it not?

2ND L. [*in the same tone of voice, nodding his head slightly in the direction of one of the other* LUNATICS]. I hear the Admiral is going to be denounced.

1ST L. [*obviously delighted*]. Oh, I'm so sorry! Poor fellow! What for?

2ND L. The usual. Byzantinism, of course: and Disaffection and Hoarding.

1ST L. Tut, tut! I should never have believed it of him!

2ND L. Oh, he's not a bad record. They say there's more than two thousand anonymous letters been written complaining about him to the Secret Police. *And all in invisible ink!*

1st L. Whew, that's nasty! [*Gleefully*]. What do you think they'll do with him?

2nd L. Send him to the Lead Mines, I expect.

1st L. [*rubbing his hands together*]. Poor fellow!

[Lunatic, *who has just fastened a flag to the end of his bed, shouts across to the* Lunatic *sitting on the bed opposite.*]

Flag-Lunatic. Hi, you! Why haven't you got your flag out? Don't you know what today is?

Lunatic without Flag. Of course I do! It's the Day of National Rejoicing.

Flag-L. Then why don't you hang out your flag? If your flag isn't out, you can't be rejoicing.

L. without F. Of course I'm rejoicing. I was just sitting rejoicing quietly by myself when you disturbed me.

Flag-L. I don't believe you're rejoicing a bit! You don't look as if you were rejoicing.

L. without F. Well, neither do you, for that matter.

Flag-L. It doesn't matter how I look. I've got my flag out. Everyone knows *I'm* rejoicing.

L. without F. What are you rejoicing about?

Flag-L. I shan't tell you. What are you?

L. without F. I shan't tell you either.

Flag-L. Oh yes you will!

L. without F. No I won't!

Flag-L. Will!

L. without F. Won't!

[*The two* Lunatics *adopt threatening attitudes and make horrible faces at each other.*]

[*A trumpet.*]

69

1st Lunatic.

Silence everybody! The Leader is going to speak
to us!

[*All the* Lunatics *stand up and give the West-
land Salute.*]

The Voice of the Leader [*through the loud-speaker
in the picture*]. A short time ago, I was spending a
week-end at a little village in the mountains. I sat
on the verandah of the simple old Westland inn,
looking out across the street to the meadows and
the mountains beyond, those snow-capped peaks
already flushed with the sunset glow. Westland
swallows swooped in and out of the eaves overhead.
In a doorway opposite, a young mother looked
down at her suckling babe with ineffable Westland
tenderness. In another, a Westland granny gazed
out into the dusk with perfect serenity on her
beautiful old face. Sturdy rosy-cheeked Westland
youngsters romped in the new-mown hay a little
further off. And presently down the street came the
returning cattle, all their bells a-chiming in a sweet
symphony, followed by the peasants, so honest, so
thrifty, so frugal, wedded to the dear Westland
earth in an eternal, holy marriage.

[*The* Lunatics *have been much affected by this
part of the speech. They sigh, shed tears and em-
brace each other with loud smacking kisses. One
of the male lunatics takes flowers from a vase and
distributes them among the ladies, who put the
flowers in their hair.*]

70

VOICE OF THE LEADER [*continuing*]. My eyes filled with tears. I could not speak just then. Perish the man, I thought, who can imagine this people capable of any base or unworthy deed! Westland! *Our* Westland! *My* Westland! All, all mine!

BUT:

A chill struck my heart. There *was* a shadow!

Not two hundred miles from where I stand, there is a Nation: trained to arms from infancy, schooled in military obedience and precision, saluting even in the cradle, splendidly equipped with every invention of modern science, able, resolute, taught to regard the individual as nothing and the State as all, scorning treaties as mere scraps of paper to be rent asunder when the interests of the State demand. My mind's eye saw the long silent grey ranks. I heard the shouting of the captains, the brazen call of the trumpet and the pawing of the chargers. And a voice said: Woe, woe to the unprepared: For their inheritance shall be taken away and their home be left desolate!

[*The* LUNATICS *are now violently agitated. Some of them moan and shiver with fear, lie flat on the floor or crawl under the beds. Others blow trumpets, wave toy swords and strike down imaginary enemies.*]

From how slight a cause may proceed terrifying results! A piece of paper left by a picnic party which has inadvertently strayed over the frontier, a rash word in a letter about the superiority of Westland beer or a humorous sketch in a revue misunderstood: and in a moment it is too late. Destruction might come upon us like a thief in the night: while you are innocently dozing in your chair, or making an omelette or washing dishes at the kitchen sink. A secret cabinet meeting, a word whispered into the telephone and within half an hour, within twenty minutes, the black hordes of death are darkening the Westland air with their horrible shadows.

Picture the scene, Oh mothers! Your baby's face, pinched and puckered: Not by hunger, no. Sated with poison from the air it breathes, its tender little mouth agape, choking up froth and green bile.

Sons, see your aged father who has taught you to reverence truth and purity: see him caught as the house collapses, his skull smashed like an egg before your eyes by a falling beam!

Think, teachers, of the bombs falling suddenly in the playing-field! There goes that splendid young forward . . . ah! he's down: collapsing even as he reaches the goal-post, his beautiful hinged limbs contracted in agony!

[*Most of the* LUNATICS *are now staring up at the ceiling in fascinated horror, as though awaiting the aeroplanes' arrival.*]

VOICE OF THE LEADER [*continuing*]. Nor is this all. The flame once lit would spread into a universal conflagration. England, Iceland, Ecuador and Siam would flare and within a week our civilisation, all that our statesmen and thinkers, our poets and musicians, have travailed for down the ages of history, would lie a smoking ruin!

No, this must not be! Westland is the guardian of Europe. We love peace (I say it in absolute confidence) more than any other country. Let us be ready and able to enforce it. We must build an air force of such a magnitude that any enemy, however ferocious, will think twice before daring to strike. Within three weeks we must have a million planes, not one less! We must make a stupendous effort. No sacrifice is too great. I expect every man, woman and child in Westland to help. Give up that cigar after lunch, do without an extra lipstick, abstain from your favourite sweets. Is that too much to ask when the safety of the Homeland is at stake? Our responsibilities are vast: Let us be worthy of them. And God help us all.

> [*Tremendous enthusiasm. The* LUNATICS *jump up and down in their delight, cheer, embrace, pillow-fight, and box each other's ears.*]

THE LUNATIC WITH THF FLAG. Let's build a great big plane for our Leader!

LUNATICS. Oh yes! Let's!!

> [*The* LUNATICS *begin dragging beds together and piling furniture upon them. The din is tremendous. Suddenly, at the window, appear the heads of the* TWO JOURNALISTS *and the* DOG. *They peer cautiously into the room, looking for* ALAN. *After a moment, they hastily withdraw.*]

73

1st Lunatic [*who evidently considers himself the most important of them all and is rather piqued that the plane-building should have been suggested by someone else, stands on a chair and begins clapping his hands to command attention; after some time, he succeeds in getting the* Lunatics *to stop working and listen to him*]. Madmen of Westland!

In this hour of supreme crisis, I feel called upon to say a few words. This is my message to you all. Let us never forget that we are Westlanders first and madmen second. As Westlanders, we have a great tradition to uphold. Westland has always produced ten per cent. more lunatics than any other country in Europe. And are we going to show ourselves inferior to our forefathers? Never!

[*The* Journalists *reappear at the window, try the strength of the bars and shake their heads. The* Dog *is seen arguing with them in dumb show and indicating that they come with him. They all disappear.*]

1st Lunatic [*continuing*]. Of recent years, there have appeared in our midst, masquerading as men of science, certain Jews, obscurantists and Marxist traitors. These men have published enormous books, attempting to provide new classifications and forms of lunacy. But we are not deceived. No foreign brand of madness, however spectacular, however noisy or pleasant, will ever seduce us from the grand old Westland Mania. What was good enough for our forefathers, we declare, is good

74

enough for us! We shall continue to go mad in the time-honoured Westland way.

A Lunatic. Three cheers for the Westland Loonies!

All. Hurrah! Hurrah! Hurrah!

Another Lunatic [*suddenly seeing* Alan]. Hullo, you! Why don't you cheer?

> [*All the* Lunatics *stop shouting and look at* Alan. *At this moment, unseen by any of them, the* Two Journalists *enter the room by a door on the right of the stage.*]

Another Lunatic. His mouth's tied up! He's got the toothache!

> [*Begins to giggle.*]

Another Lunatic. He's been sent here to spy on us !

Another. He's been hoarding butter!

Another. He's insulted the Leader!

Another. Rumour-monger!

Another. Non-Aryan!

Another. Separatist!

Another. Grumbler!

> [*All this time, they draw closer to him, rushing forward in turns to tug at his hair, tweak his nose or pull his ears.*]

A Lunatic. Squirt water at him!

Another. Put a rat in his bed!

Another. Tickle his toes!

Another. Shave off his eyebrows!

Another. I say, chaps! Let's do something really exciting! Let's put lavatory paper under his chair and burn it!

[*They seem about to make a final rush at* ALAN, *when the* 1ST JOURNALIST *speaks, in a very loud and impressive voice, like a conjurer.*]

1ST J. Ladies and Gentlemen! [*All the* LUNATICS *turn round to stare at him.*] I am about to show you a simple but extremely interesting scientific experiment. [*Holds up his hand.*] Now, watch the duck's head and please keep absolutely still while I count a hundred. One. Two. Three. . . .

[*While the* 1ST JOURNALIST *is counting, the* 2ND JOURNALIST, *on all fours, worms his way through the crowd to* ALAN'S *side and begins hastily undoing the ropes and straps.*]

2ND J. [*in a low voice, to* ALAN]. Gosh, that was a close shave!

ALAN. How on earth did you find me?

2ND J. Your Dog guided us here. That animal is better than the whole of Scotland Yard put together. He's outside now, keeping guard over the warders until we get you loose. . . . Curse these knots!

[*Meanwhile, the* 1ST J. *continues to count. But the* LUNATICS *are becoming less attentive. Those who are standing close to* ALAN *begin to take an interest in the* 2ND JOURNALIST'S *activities.*]

LUNATIC.
What are you doing that for?

2ND J. Can't you see? I'm tying him up tighter. The ropes had got loose. See this one? [*He holds it up.*] It had slipped right off. [*He throws it away.*] No good at all.

76

[*He continues to unfasten the other ropes and straps.*]

LUNATIC. I'll help you.

[*Begins to refasten the straps.*]

2ND J. Don't bother, old boy. I can manage by myself.

[*Unfastens them again.*]

LUNATIC. It's no bother. I like helping people. I'm a Boy Scout.

2ND J. Well, do your day's good deed by leaving me alone, see?

LUNATIC. I don't think that would be a good deed, would it?

2ND J. You bet it would!

LUNATIC. Perhaps you're right. But I'd better just ask the others what they think. [*In a very loud voice.*] I say! [*All the* LUNATICS *turn round to look at him.*]

2ND J. Holy Moses, that's torn it!

1ST LUNATIC. What are you doing with our prisoner?

2ND L. Where's your warrant?

3RD L. Habeas Corpus!

4TH L. It's a rescue!

5TH L. Stand by the doors!

OTHERS. Fire! Murder! Treason!

[*The* 1ST JOURNALIST, *now disregarded, rushes to the Leader's picture and gets behind it.*]

1ST J. [*through the loud-speaker*]. Company! Fall in!

[*The* LUNATICS *immediately form a double rank, facing the Leader's picture.* 2ND J. *continues feverishly with the work of untying* ALAN.]

1st J. Slooope Hyppp!

> [*The* LUNATICS *go through the motion of sloping arms.*]

1st J. Oddah Hyppp!

> [LUNATICS *order arms.*]

1st J. Slooope Hyppp! [*They do so.*] Oddah Hyppp!
> [*They do so.*]

2nd J. [*to* ALAN]. That's all the drill he knows! [*Undoing the last strap.*] There! Come on, this is where we scoot!

> [*They rush out.*]

1st J. Company! Man the aeroplane! Fall out!

> [*The* LUNATICS *rush to the structure of beds and scramble upon it. The* 1st JOURNALIST *slips from behind the picture and runs out after the others.*]

1st LUNATIC. Start her up!

> [*The* LUNATICS *imitate the roaring of the engines.*]

1st L. Off we go! Faster! Faster! She's left the ground! We're rising! Higher! Higher!

> [*The* LUNATICS *wave their handkerchiefs and grimace at the audience.*]

A MAD LADY. Isn't the view gorgeous?

2nd MAD LADY. Look, there's the asylum. Just a tiny little speck!

A MAD LADY. I'll spit down the chimney!

> [*Spits.*]

THE PILOT. Hold on tight! I'm going to loop the loop!

78

[*Shrieks of dismay. The* LUNATICS *heave the beds up on end until the whole structure collapses. General confusion.* ALAN, *the* JOURNALISTS *and the* DOG *peep in for a moment at the window and disappear laughing.*]

CURTAIN

CHORUS

Paddington. King's Cross. Euston. Liverpool Street:

Each hiding behind a gothic hotel its gigantic green-
house

And the long trains groomed before dawn departing at
ten,

Picking their way through slums between the washing
and the privies

To a clear run through open country,

Ignoring alike the cathedral towns in their wide femi-
nine valleys, and the lonely junctions.

In such a train sit Norman and his dog

Moving backwards through Westland at a mile a minute

And playing hearts with their two friends on an open
mackintosh:

Picture the Pullman car with its deft attendants

And the usual passengers: the spoilt child, the corridor
addict,

The lady who expects you to admire her ankles: the
ostentatious peruser of important papers, etc. etc.

They have been travelling all day, it is late afternoon.

Outside the windows of the warm sealed tube, as a back-
ground to their conversation,

Imagine a hedgeless country, the source of streams;
Such as the driver, changing up at last, sees stretching
    from Hartside east and south,
Deadstones above Redan, Thackmoss, Halfpenny Scar,
Two Top and Muska, Pity Mea, Bullpot Brow:
Land of the ring ousel: a bird stone-haunting, an un-
    quiet bird.

SCENE II

[*In a railway-train.* ALAN, *the* TWO JOURNALISTS *and the* DOG *are playing cards. A little distance off sits the* FINANCIER, *at present half hidden by his newspaper.*]

1ST J. Your lead, Alan.

[ALAN *plays.*] [1ST J. *plays a card.*]

ALAN [*to* 2ND J.]. Eight to beat.

2ND J. [*looking at* DOG]. Hm . . . shall I risk it? No, I don't think so.

[*He plays a card. The* DOG *also plays a card.*]

1ST J. [*suspiciously*]. Hullo, you short-suited? Here, let's see your hand.

[*He reaches out to take the* DOG'S *cards. The* DOG *growls and refuses to show them.*]

ALAN. Show them to me, Francis. Good Dog! [DOG *reluctantly hands over the cards.*] But you've got Slippery Anne here, look!

2ND J. Darned if he hasn't been cheating again.

ALAN [*indignantly*]. He wasn't cheating! He just doesn't understand the rules, do you Doggy?

1ST J. If you ask me, that Dog of yours understands a damn sight too much. He's too smart by half. [*Yawns.*] Well, gentlemen, you've cleaned me out.

I'll go and stretch myself a bit. [*Standing up, he catches sight of the* FINANCIER: *sits down abruptly: to* 2ND J., *in a whisper.*] Great God, man, look!

2ND J. Where?

1ST J. There!

2ND J. Snakes! It isn't . . . ?

1ST J. Bet you a fiver it is!

2ND J. The papers say he's in Manchukuo.

1ST J. Just eyewash!

2ND J. Boy! I believe you're right!

ALAN [*loudly*]. What's all the fuss about!

1ST J. Ssh!

2ND J. Sssh!!

ALAN. You might tell a fellow!

1ST J. [*stage whisper*]. Grabstein! Sitting just behind you!

ALAN. Grabstein?

2ND J. Ssh!

ALAN. Who's he when he's at home?

1ST J. Oh boy, where were you educated? [*Wearily, to* 2ND J.] Go on, you tell him.

2ND J. President of the X.Y.Z.

1ST J. Chairman of the Pan-Asiatic.

2ND J. Practically owns South America.

1ST J. The biggest crook in Europe. Got his finger in everything. Whatever happens, he's in on the ground floor. Why, he even gets to hear of things before *we* do, sometimes!

ALAN. I say! Not really! I wonder if he knows where Francis is?

83

2ND J. Most likely he does. The question is: would he tell you?

1ST J. [winking at 2ND J.]. Go and ask him.

ALAN. Shall I really?

2ND J. [winking at 1ST J.]. Atta boy!

ALAN [doubtfully]. All right. . . . If you don't think he'd mind?

1ST J. Hell! Why should he?

2ND J. He'll welcome you with open arms.

1ST J. [artfully]. By the way, you might ask him a few other questions while you're about it. Find out what holdings he has in Sahara Electrics.

2ND J. And how much it cost him to start the war in Spitsbergen?

1ST J. And what became of the Cloaguan Prime Minister after the Platinum Scandals?

ALAN. I say, hold on a minute: I shall never remember all that! Just give me time to write it down.

> [He takes a piece of paper from his pocket and makes notes. The JOURNALISTS whisper instructions into his ear.]

ALAN. But won't he think me awfully inquisitive?

2ND J. Oh, he loves being asked questions. . . . Just go up to him and say: 'Potts'. That's the name of a very dear friend of his. It'll put him in a good temper at once.

ALAN [doubtfully]. Righto.

> [He approaches the FINANCIER. The JOURNALISTS shake hands with each other in ecstasies of delight.]

1st J. Oh boy, I wouldn't have missed this for a thousand pounds!

> [*During the following scene, the* JOURNALISTS *take photographs and make notes.*]

ALAN [*rather nervously*]. Potts.

> [*The* FINANCIER *looks up from his newspaper, stares at him for a moment, turns deadly pale. Then, with a shrug of his shoulders, he takes a cheque-book from his pocket and unscrews the cap of his fountain-pen.*]

FINANCIER [*with a deep sigh*]. How much do you want?

ALAN. I beg your pardon, sir. I don't quite understand.

FINANCIER [*more firmly*]. I'll give you a thousand: Not one penny more. And you understand that I'm doing it because I don't choose to be annoyed at this particular moment. I have reasons for remaining incognito. I suppose you counted on that? Very well. . . . But let me warn you, if you're fool enough to imagine that you can play this game twice, you were never more mistaken. I have ways of dealing with gentry of your sort. Understand?

ALAN. I'm awfully sorry, sir. But I think you must be making some mistake. . . . I only wanted to ask you a few questions. . . . It's frightful cheek of me, I know. . . .

FINANCIER. Oh, a journalist, eh? That's bad enough. Still, as you're here, I suppose I can let you have five minutes. Ask away. . . .

ALAN [*consulting his notes*]. First of all, did you forge

the report on the diamond mines on Tuesday Island?

[*The* FINANCIER *gasps*.]

ALAN [*continuing hurriedly*]. Secondly, is it true that you staged the fake attempt on the Prince of the Hellespont in order to corner the rubber market?

FINANCIER. Do you seriously expect me to answer that?

ALAN. Well, no sir. To be quite candid, I don't. Please don't be angry. . . . Thirdly, did you have the men murdered who were going to show up the Bishop of Pluvium?

FINANCIER [*laughs*]. Young man, you amuse me. Very well, since you're the first newspaper man who's ever dared to talk to me like this, I'll tell you the truth. The answer to all your three questions is: 'Yes. I did.' There! Now you've got a grand story, haven't you? Go and ask your editor to print it and he'll kick you out into the street. What's your paper, by the way? Ten to one, I own it.

ALAN. The Pressan Ambo Parish Magazine.

FINANCIER. Never heard of it. But I'll buy it to-morrow, lock stock and barrel. How much would your boss take, do you suppose?

ALAN. I'm afraid I couldn't tell you that, sir. You see, I only write for it occasionally. A bit of poetry now and then. Awful rot, I expect you'd think it.

FINANCIER [*groans*]. Good God! Don't say you're a poet too!

ALAN. Oh rather not, sir!

FINANCIER. Glad to hear it. Of course, mind you, I've nothing against poets, provided they make good. They say that one or two fellows at the top of the tree are earning as much as four thousand a year. I doubt it myself.... But the fact remains that most of them are moral degenerates or Bolsheviks, or both. The scum of the earth. My son's a poet.

ALAN. I'm sorry, sir.

FINANCIER [*sentimentally*]. It's been the greatest disappointment of my whole life. Who have I got to work for, to be proud of? Nobody. And my wife encourages him; the bitch. As long as she's got her cocaine and her gigolos, we can all go to hell as far as she's concerned.... I don't know why I'm telling you all this.

ALAN [*politely*]. It's rotten luck for you, sir.

FINANCIER. Look here. I've taken a fancy to you. Will you be my secretary? Starting at five thousand a year, with all extras. Yes or no?

ALAN. It's most awfully kind of you, sir: but I'm afraid I can't....

FINANCIER [*emotionally*]. There, you see! I knew it! You don't like me. None of them like me. Wherever I go I see it. I can't so much as get a really friendly smile out of a railway-porter, though Heaven knows I tip them enough....

[*Sings. Accompaniment by dining-car attendant with gong.*]

When I was young I showed such application,
    I worked the whole day long;
I hoped to rise above my station,
    To rise just like a song:
I did so want to be a hero
    In just a rich man's way
But I might just as well be Nero,
    And this is all I have to say:

CHORUS [*with* ATTENDANT *and* JOURNALISTS].

        Why are they so rude to me?
        It seems so crude to me,
        I want to be friendly
        But it's no good, for
        No one has love for me,
        Only a shove for me,
        They bait me and hate me, I'm
        Misunderstood.

FINANCIER.

        I've founded hospitals and rest-homes,
            Subscribed to public funds,
        Promoted schemes for planning Best Homes
            And built a school for nuns.
        I've studied all the Italian Masters,
            I've tried to read French books,
         But all my efforts seem disasters:
            I only get such nasty looks.

CHORUS.

        Why are they so rude to me, . . . etc.

FINANCIER. Now what is it? Tell me straight out; don't be afraid. Is it my face? Is it my voice? Is it my manner? Or are you all just jealous of my damned money?

ALAN. It isn't that, sir. Really it isn't. But you see . . . I'm not free. I've got a kind of job . . . if you can call it a job. . . .

FINANCIER. Chuck it. I'll give you six thousand.

ALAN. You see, sir, it's not that kind of job: that you can chuck up, I mean. . . . I've got to look for someone. He's Sir Francis Crewe, Bart. At least, he's Bart if he's alive. . . . That's what I really came to ask you about. . . . He ran away from home ten years ago. I thought you might happen to know where he is.

FINANCIER. What do you take me for? A nursemaid?

[*The train stops. A* PORTER *looks in at the window.*]

PORTER. All change for Malaga, Reykjavik and Omsk!

FINANCIER. I must get out here. Will you take ten thousand? Yes or no? It's my last word.

ALAN. I'm truly most terribly sorry, but. . . .

FINANCIER. You're more of a fool than I took you for. [*Sentimentally*]. Write to me sometimes and tell me how you're getting on. It would be so lovely to get a letter which had nothing to do with business!

ALAN. Rather, sir!

FINANCIER. Oh, by the way, a good place to look for that Baronet of yours would be Paradise Park. This train'll take you there. It's where most wasters and

cranks land up sooner or later, if they've still got
some cash to be swindled out of. You'll meet my
dear son, among others. Perhaps you'll be able to
knock some sense into him. Tell him I offer him a
hundred thousand if he'll stop writing his drivel
and clean a sewer. Goodbye.

ALAN. Goodbye, sir. Thanks awfully.

> [*The* FINANCIER, *with the help of* ALAN *and
> the* PORTER, *descends from the train.*]

1ST J. [*to* 2ND J.]. Quick, we mustn't lose sight of him!
If we follow him now, maybe we'll get the dope on
that Dripping Merger, after all!

> [*They leave the train.*]

2ND J. [*to* ALAN]. You coming, Kid?

ALAN. I can't. I'm afraid. I've just got a new clue.

1ST J. Well, good luck.

2ND J. Ta ta.

ALAN. Goodbye, and thanks most awfully for all you've
done.

> [*The train moves on.* ALAN *waves from the
> window. Then he turns to the* DOG.]

ALAN. Well, Doggy. We're all alone, now. Just you and
me. [*He puts his arm round the* DOG's *neck.*] I
wonder what Iris is doing? Oh dear, I wish we
weren't such a long way from home. . . .

> [*He gazes sadly out of the window.*]

CURTAIN

CHORUS

Happy the hare at morning, for she cannot read
The Hunter's waking thoughts. Lucky the leaf
Unable to predict the fall. Lucky indeed
The rampant suffering suffocating jelly
Burgeoning in pools, lapping the grits of the desert,
The elementary sensual cures,
The hibernations and the growth of hair assuage:
Or best of all the mineral stars disintegrating quietly
    into light.
But what shall man do, who can whistle tunes by heart,
Know to the bar when death shall cut him short, like the
    cry of the shearwater?
We will show you what he has done.
How comely are his places of refuge and the tabernacles
    of his peace,
The new books upon the morning table, the lawns and
    the afternoon terraces!
Here are the playing-fields where he may forget his ig-
    norance
To operate within a gentleman's agreement: twenty-two
    sins have here a certain licence.
Here are the thickets where accosted lovers combattant
May warm each other with their wicked hands,

Here are the avenues for incantation and workshops for
the cunning engravers.

The galleries are full of music, the pianist is storming the
keys, the great cellist is crucified over his instru-
ment,

That none may hear the ejaculations of the sentinels

Nor the sigh of the most numerous and the most poor;
the thud of their falling bodies

Who with their lives have banished hence the serpent
and the faceless insect.

SCENE III

[*The gardens of Paradise Park. A beautifully-kept lawn.
Numbers of people are walking about the stage in sports
clothes of various kinds or propelling themselves hither and
thither in invalid chairs. Some lie on the grass absorbed in
books. In the background are two large trees. In one of the
trees sits the* POET, *smoking cigarettes: In the other are
two* LOVERS *dressed in nursery-teapot-Dutch costumes. In
the distance, the band plays a waltz.*]

CHORUS. When you're in trouble,
    When you get the air,
  When everything returns your ring
    Do not despair, because although
  Friends may forsake you
    And all skies are dark
You can be gay if you just step this way
    Into Paradise Park.

  Was it a tiring day
    On your office stool?
Has your wife all your life
    Made you feel a fool? Don't cry, for though
Landlords perplex you
    And all bosses frown,

93

> In Paradise Park you can feel a young spark
> And do them down!

[*Enter* ALAN *and the* DOG. *They approach the* POET'S *tree.*]

ALAN [*to* POET]. Excuse me, sir. Is this Paradise Park?

POET. ἔστιν θάλασσα, τίς δέ νιν κατασβέσαι.

ALAN. I beg your pardon?

POET. Nil nimium studeo, Caesar, tibi velle placere nec scire utrum sis albus aut ater homo.

ALAN. I'm awfully sorry, but I don't understand. Do you speak English?

POET. Nessun maggior dolore che ricordarsi del tempo felice.

ALAN. I know a little German, if that will do. . . . Entschuldigen Sie, bitte. Koennen Sie mir sagen, ob dies ist der Garten von Paradies?

POET. Dans l'an trentième de mon age. . . . [ALAN *begins to move off.*] Oh well, if you insist on talking our filthy native language, I suppose I must. . . . Give me a cigarette. I've finished mine.

ALAN. I'm so sorry. . . . Of course. . . .
> Is the name Sir Francis Crewe
> Known by any chance to you?

POET. Did you like it?

ALAN. Er . . . ?

POET. I'm so glad you did! I wrote it!

ALAN. Wrote what?

POET. 'Advances New', of course. Now tell me, which section did you like the best? *Mandrake* is the best technically, of course. But *Cinders* is more the real me, I think.

ALAN. I'm afraid you misunderstood me. I said Sir Francis Crewe. I've been looking for him.

POET. 'Your chase had a beast in view.'

ALAN. You know where he is?

POET. Well, of course.

ALAN. Where?

POET [*tapping his forehead*]. Here. Everything's here. You're here. He's here. This park's here. This tree's here. If I shut my eyes they all disappear.

ALAN. And what happens if I shut *my* eyes? Do you disappear, too?

POET [*crossly*]. No, of course not! I'm the only real person in the whole world.

ALAN. Well, suppose your tree was cut down? It wouldn't be there when you looked for it.

POET. Nonsense! The axe wouldn't exist unless I thought of it. The woodcutter wouldn't exist either.

ALAN. Isn't your Father the famous financier?

POET. I used to think so. But I got tired of that and forgot him. Give me another cigarette.

[*As he leans down, the* DOG *jumps up and bites his hand.*]

POET [*nursing his hand*]. Why can't you keep your blasted dog in order? Oh, my poor hand!

ALAN. I'm most dreadfully sorry. But you see, he's never seen a real person before. When you're only an imaginary dog and have been eating imaginary biscuits all your life, a real hand must taste simply

95

delicious. You couldn't resist it, could you, Francis
old boy? [*To* POET]. Never mind. Just shut your
eyes and you'll forget all about us.

POET [*with his eyes shut*]. Oh, I've forgotten *you* long
ago! It's my hand I keep remembering!

      [ALAN *and* DOG *move on to the* LOVERS' *tree.*]

1ST LOVER. Little white dove, it's you that I love,

    Fairer than hollyhocks far!

    How nice and how neat

    Are your dear little feet!

    You make my heart beat!

    How terribly sweet, how terribly sweet,

    How terribly sweet you are!

     [*They hug each other, taking no notice of* ALAN.]

ALAN. Excuse me, please, disturbing you:

    But have you heard of Sir Francis Crewe?

2ND L. Have you, darling?

1ST L. Oh, pretty starling!

    Say that again

    And again and again!

    I love to watch your cheek

    Move when you speak!

2ND L. Oh dearest, you mustn't go on so!

    There's a nice man down below

    And there is something he wants to know.

1ST L. Good morning. Let me introduce my wife.

    We're going to be lovers all our life:

    Two as one and one as two.

    Is there anything we can do?

ALAN. Have you heard of Sir Francis Crewe?

1st L. Sir Francis Crewe? Do *you* know, sweet?

Was that the funny old man on the seat

Who looked so cross when I gave you a kiss?

2nd L. You were so naughty! Oh!

1st L. [*embracing her*].   Just like this!

ALAN. No, he's not very old.

1st L. Darling, you're cold.

Put my coat on. What dear little shoulders!

[ALAN *begins to move off.*]

Don't go, old man. You mustn't scold us.

We'd ask you up, but there isn't room.

But when we've a large tree you must come.

[ALAN *moves off.*]

2nd L. Wonderful boy, you're all my joy!

1st L. I'd like to eat you for tea!

2nd L. You're so tender and strong!

1st L. You're just like a song!

2nd L. To you I belong!

BOTH. You cannot do wrong, you cannot do wrong,

You cannot do wrong with me!

[*Two* FEMALE INVALIDS *in bath-chairs move
to the front of the stage.*]

1st INVALID. How many stitches have you got?

2nd I. [*proudly*]. Four.

1st I. Oh do let me see!

2nd I. Not now, wait till the dressing.

1st I. Oh please! Just one peep!

2nd I. Very well.

[*Shows wound.*]

1st I. Oh, what a beauty!

2ND I. Don't tell Alice. Promise! She's terribly jealous. They only put two in her. When they told her after she'd come round, she cried.

1ST I. Betty's a lucky girl. She's got tubes.

2ND I. She hasn't!

1ST I. Yes! Only it's a secret. She told me all about it at breakfast. My dear, they took out *everything*! She even thinks they may give her a real silver set!

2ND I. How too marvellous! Won't her Ted be proud?

ALAN [*approaching them*]. Excuse me.
    Is the name Sir Francis Crewe
    Known perhaps to either of you?

1ST I. What's he got?

ALAN. Got?

1ST I. What illness has he got?

ALAN. What? Is he ill?

1ST I. Of course he is, silly: if he's here. Aren't you?

ALAN. No. I don't think so.

BOTH INVALIDS [*turning their chairs away*]. How disgusting!

    [*Enter a* COLONEL *in a bath-chair, with an ear-trumpet.*]

ALAN. Excuse me, sir, but is Sir Francis Crewe
    Known by any chance to you?

COLONEL. Can't hear a word, sir. Stone deaf, thank God!

    [ALAN *wanders off asking various other people. The two* INVALIDS *return.*]

1ST I. Have you ever noticed his hands? Just like a violinist's.

2ND I. I wonder who he'll chose for the operation today?

1ST I. [*blushing*]. Well, I don't like to be presumptuous, but I think . . . .

2ND I. No? Not really!

1ST I. [*complacent*]. Hm, hm. . . .

2ND I. My dear, I *do* congratulate you!

1ST I. It was only a look, mind you: but you can't mistake him when he looks at you like that. Made me feel quite goosey! Oh look, there he is coming out of the ward! Quickly, dear, lend me your powder-puff. I must look my best when I go under. . . . Ooh, the brute! He's chosen that new case! It isn't fair!

[*Bursts into tears.*]

2ND I. There, there, darling! Don't take on so! It's sure to be you next time.

1ST I. [*blubbering*]. I don't care! I was counting on it today. It's too bad! He only came in this morning.

[*The* INVALIDS *move away as the* SURGEON *and* ANAESTHETIST *enter, followed by a* NURSE *pushing* CHIMP EAGLE, *the patient, on a wheeled stretcher.*]

SUR. What do you think, Doctor! Intraspinal or general?

AN. Oh, general in this case.

SUR. You're playing on Saturday, aren't you?

AN. Yes, I hope so.

SUR. Good man! We can't do without you in the deep. Young Waters is playing too. He's no snyde at the game.

[*Exeunt* SURGEON *and* ANAESTHETIST.]

99

CHIMP EAGLE [*recognizing* ALAN]. Hullo, Alan!

ALAN. Why, it's Chimp Eagle! What's the matter with you, old man?

CHIMP. A strike down at the Docks. The Police had a machine-gun. Got me in the guts. . . . I say, you aren't in with our lot too, are you?

ALAN. No, I'm looking for Francis.

CHIMP. Francis: The missing heir! [*Smiles.*] How long ago that seems. I'd forgotten all about him.

ALAN. Chimp . . . did you ever find out anything?

CHIMP. I can't remember. . . . No. . . . That is, yes. . . . I. . . .

[*He is too exhausted to say more.*]

NURSE [*coming forward*]. Now then, sir: That's enough. You're tiring the patient.

ALAN [*withdrawing to the other side of stage, to* DOG]. Oh Doggy, what shall I do? They're coming to take him away. And I *must* speak to him again some-how. . . . Oh dear . . . !

[*The* DOG *gives* ALAN *a glance, as much as to say: Watch me! Then it runs across the stage and begins fawning on the* NURSE]

NURSE. What a lovely doggie! May I pat him? [*The* DOG *jumps at her and begins tearing off her uniform.*] Oh! Oh! Help!

ALAN. What on earth are you doing? Naughty dog! Stop it this minute! [*Suddenly understanding.*] No, don't stop! Splendid! Good dog! I'll help.

[*They strip the* NURSE *of her uniform and tie her up. The* DOG *is dressed by* ALAN *in the*

Nurse's *uniform. They dump the* Nurse *in a disused bath-chair and cover her with a rug. Scarcely are they ready when the* Surgeon *returns.*]

Sur. Nurse, what the Dickens are you waiting for? Bring the patient at once, please.

[*The* Dog *wheels* Chimp Eagle *out.* Alan *follows at a discreet distance.*]

Chorus. There's consolations here to suit
        Every mood and means:
     Skating-rinks, booths for drinks,
       Gambling-machines and switchbacks and
     Art for the Highbrow
      And Sport for the Low-:
     Life is a lark at Paradise Park;
      For the fast and the slow.

CURTAIN

CHORUS

Seeding and harvest, the mating of lions, the divergent
    migrations are themes for another occasion than this:
In this white world of order and professional attentions
Of airy wards, the smell of iodoform, the squeak of
    rubber tyred stretchers
Solar time is unreal.
Against these walls the waves of action and charity
    must wash in vain.

1600 beds
10 theatres magnificently equipped
A special wing for infectious cases
A chapel, a mortuary, labs for research, and really ade-
    quate nursing accommodation
And, opened last year, a solarium for the convalescent.

1600 beds: in each one patient, apparently alone;
One who has forsaken family and friends; to set up
    house here with his hostile shadow.
You who are amorous and active, pause here an instant.
See passion transformed into rheumatism; rebellion
    into paralysis; power into a tumour.
That which was hated, became hateful; that which was
    creative, a stalking destruction; that which was
    loving, a tormenting flame
For those who reject their gifts: choose here their pun-
    ishment.

SCENE IV

[*Paradise Park. The operating theatre. Railed off, at the side of the stage, are benches for students. Two* STUDENTS *are already seated there. The theatre itself is empty.*]

1ST STUDENT. But surely you know that one?

2ND S. Is it about the Italian and the two goats?

1ST S. No, no. This is about a man who wanted to buy a bird-cage. . . .

[*Whispers.*]

. . . He said: There's a stigma
About the letter sigma. . . .

2ND S. [*laughing*]. That's damn good! Damn good, that is!

[ALAN *enters shyly and sits down in the corner, looking round him.*]

1ST S. [*indicating* ALAN]. Who's that johnny? Don't know him.

2ND S. A sweat-pot from one of the other hospitals, probably.

1ST S. [*to* ALAN]. Hullo. Are you from St Gag's?

ALAN [*nervously*]. Er, yes.

1ST S. What did you score this afternoon against Bullocks'?

2ND S. Who's batting?

ALAN. Er, I think. . . .

> [*At this moment, a* 3RD STUDENT *comes in. He is struggling to get a white coat over his dinner-jacket.*]

3RD S. Thank God I'm not late! The old man had it in for me today.

2ND S. Hullo, Sandy. Were you at the Boat Club Supper?

3RD S. Was I not! Just my luck to have to leave when things were getting lively! They're just starting to wreck the hall. Fatty's smashed his collar-bone already and Roy's lost a tooth. It's going to be a ripping rag.

1ST S. Let's hope this case doesn't take long. [*Turning to* ALAN.] By the way, what did you say the score was?

2ND S. Ssh! They're coming!

> [*An harmonium begins to play a voluntary. The* STUDENTS *and* ALAN *rise to their feet. Procession of* NURSES (*including* DOG), DRESSERS, *the* PATIENT *on his stretcher,* ANAESTHETIST *and* SURGEON. *The* SURGEON *takes up a position at the end of the table with his back to the audience. The note is given. ff subito. Flavour of Bach in his dramatic mood.*]

ALL STUDENTS [*heavy 4-part harmony*].

> We see death every day
> But do not understand him.

SUR. I believe

ALL. in the physical causation of all phenomena, material or mental: and in the germ theory of disease. And in Hippocrates, the father of Medicine, Galen, Ambrose Paré, Liston of the enormous hands, Syme, Lister who discovered the use of antiseptics, Hunter and Sir Frederick Treves.

And I believe in surgical treatment for duodenal ulcer, cerebral abscess, pyloric stenosis, aneurism and all forms of endocrine disturbance.

SUR. Let not the patient react unfavourably to the anaesthetic.

ALL. But let it save him from pain.

SUR. Let there be no unforeseen complications.

ALL. Neither let sepsis have the advantage.

SUR. May my skill not desert me.

ALL. But guide your hands.

SUR. Gentlemen, we have before us a case of abdominal injury, caused by a bullet piercing the bowel. I intend therefore to make a five-inch median incision, dividing the Rectus Abdominus, bring the bowel forward, resect it, wash out the peritoneum with warm saline and insert a tube for drainage. Is it clear?

ALL. It is.

[SURGEON *turns to wash his hands. During this process, the* STUDENTS *sing the following C of E, chant.*]

DEC. The surgeon is great: Let his name appear in the birthday honours.

CAN. I was in danger of death: And he delivered me:

Dec. I was in fever and I could not sleep: The pain assailed me all day long.

Can. I groaned in the darkness: I was in terror for my life: I took no pleasure in women, neither in the innocent pastimes of children, my food had lost its flavour.

Dec. The physicians shook their heads: they consulted together in the next room and were perplexed.

Can. They prescribed diets, carthartics, drugs and all manner of salves and ointments: but no one of them relieved me.

Unison. But the surgeon, he relieved me: he removed the emphasis of my trouble and I was healed.

Surgeon [*adjusting his gloves and picking up a scalpel*]. It's a terrible thing, nurse, to keep wicket for a man's life.

Alan.   Who's the surgeon?

1st Student. Sir William Spurgeon,
                The famous amateur cricketer:
                He captained the Hospital's team last
                year.

Other Students. Ssh!
                [*Roll of drums, as if before a tight-rope act in the circus. The* Surgeon *begins to operate. Suddenly the lights go out.*]

Surgeon. Lights! Nurse! Dresser! You dresser next to that damned dresser! For God's sake get a torch! Light, give me a bloody light! Christ, is there no one in this bloody theatre who understands plain

106

English? Someone go and find out what it's all about.

[*Electric torches are brought. One of the* NURSES *goes out.*]

SURGEON. Scalpel, nurse. Not that one, idiot! Forceps. More forceps! More! More! More!

I have cut the mesenteric!

Death has declared!

[*Throws instruments about the room.*]

ANAESTHETIST. He's sinking, sir. I'd better give him an injection of adrenalin.

SURGEON [*to* DRESSER]. God man, don't chatter! Do something! How the Hell do you think I can see if you stand a mile away? Hold the torch nearer! Get out of my way!

SISTER [*returning*]. It was the Boat Club, Sir William. They're having a supper tonight, you know. One of the students fused the lights. He says he's very sorry. They'll be on again in a few minutes.

SURGEON. Oh, he's sorry, is he? That's good. That's very good. I'll make him sorry he was ever born. I'll break him! I'll break the Hospital Boat! I'll have rowing forbidden in this Hospital for ever!

[*He utters a terrible roar and rushes out.*]

3RD STUDENT. Just our luck! If it had been his precious cricketers, he'd have been as meek as a lamb.

A NURSE. Something's the matter. The patient's coming to! Holy Mother of all the Saints, have mercy!

[CHIMP EAGLE *sits up. The music of the en-*

107

CHIMP.   O Pressan Fells
    How beautiful you are!
I hear your bells
    Alas I cannot come
To Pressan home:
    I have wandered too far.

CHORUS.   (Pain makes him wander in his mind,
There's nothing audible of any kind.)

ALAN.   O my Eagle!

CHIMP.   I hear a voice
    That makes me rejoice.
Who is it standing there?
    I cannot see you clear.

ALAN.   Eagle, it is I,
    Alan Norman standing by.

CHIMP.   I cannot see.
    Twixt you and me
Death's great tired face
    Hangs in space.

CHORUS.   (Death makes him wander in his mind,
There's nothing visible of any kind.)

ALAN.   I am near.
Do not fear.

CHIMP.   She gives me loving glances.

ALAN.   Where is Francis?

CHIMP.   When the Midget died
I was by his side.
He said to me then

108

Out of his pain:
'Return again
To England. I swear
That Francis is there.'
But I forgot
My choice and lot.
More I cannot tell.
Darkness assails me and I fail:
Farewell.

ALAN. O Eagle stay.
I will take you home.

CHIMP. Nay, death has come.
She beckons me away.
Beasts and flowers are in her keeping,
In her arms I would be sleeping.

ALAN. You shall not die!

CHIMP. No, Alan, no.
The surgeon now
Is ignorant as a dove.
To Iris my love.

[*Dies.*]

[*The lights go on again. The* SURGEON *comes in.*]

SUR. That's settled 'em, I think. . . . Well, Sister, how's the patient?

SISTER. The patient is dead, Sir William.

SUR. Dead! How dare you let him die? Great God, couldn't a dozen of you keep him alive for five minutes? This is the sort of thing which invariably happens whenever my back is turned. Typical.

Typical. . . . What about this injection you gave the patient? Show me the bottle. [NURSE *gives it him.*] And you can look me in the face and say you thought this was Adrenalin? Why, you blind miserable cow, this is hydrochloric acid!

SISTER [*in tears*]. The new probationer gave it me, Sir William.

SURGEON. The new probationer, eh? This is becoming amusing! Bring me the new probationer.

[*The* NURSES *push the* DOG *forward.*]

SURGEON. So you're the culprit, eh? Well, let me tell you, my good girl, if I ever see you in this theatre again, I'll . . . .

[*He becomes aware that he is staring into a* DOG's *face. There is an awful pause. The* SURGEON *makes some inarticulate sounds as if about to have a fit. The* DOG *utters a long-drawn howl. Then it turns and bolts for the door, its cap flying from its head. General dismay, confusion, screams, laughter, pursuit.* ALAN *rushes out after the others.*]

CURTAIN

110

SCENE V

[*Night. The Highroad. In the middle of the stage stands a milestone.*]

CHORUS. Night. And crooked Europe hidden in shadow:
The Rhine catching the moonlight for hundreds of
  miles, watched by lovers:
Night in England: Over Lincolnshire and the great
  churches:
Glimpses of the constellations between their pinnacles
  and flying buttresses:
And here Alan and his companion, on foot on road, a
  forest on either side:
A strong moon pitches their shadows forward:
Sounds of their footsteps break against the woody
  masses
But the tide in the tall trees is taciturn, another
  life:
Alan lifting his eyes sees The Bear, the Waggoner, the
  Scales
And Algol waxing and waning as his hope, no life at
  all.

[*Enter* ALAN *and* DOG.]

111

ALAN.   Night has fallen, we have lost our way.
             You are tired and so am I.
         Let us wait till it is day.
             Against this milestone let us lie
         And sleep as best we may.
                 [*They both lie down behind the milestone.*]

CHORUS. Dear Sleep, the secretary of that strange club
    Where all are members upon one condition,
    That they forget their own importance;
    Where Lord and Link-Boy leave themselves with
        others
    And night after night for nothing are refreshed:
    May our names from your register never be struck off!
                 [*Enter, from behind the milestone*, ALAN'S
                 LEFT *and* RIGHT FOOT. *The* RIGHT FOOT
                 speaks in a cultured voice, the LEFT FOOT *has
                 a Cockney accent.*] *

RIGHT FOOT. Why are you pushing me, Left?

LEFT F. Cos yer tiking up all the room, that's why.

RIGHT F. Well, that's no reason to push. Pushing
    won't make things better for either of us.

LEFT F. It's bleedin' cold. Scratch me back for me, will
    yer, Right? Naow, a bit 'igher up.

RIGHT F. Is that better?

LEFT F. That's fine. Hell, I'm tired!

RIGHT F. So am I. It's been a tiring day.

LEFT F. I always feels tired now. Proper done in. The
    cramp keeps gettin' me. It gets me bad, some-
    times.

* In a performance the ensuing dialogue should probably be cut.

112

RIGHT F. You ought to see a doctor.

LEFT F. Corse I ort. But the Boss won't let me. Jest let 'im wyte. One o' these dys I'll 'ave 'is guts fer garters.

RIGHT F. I don't think you should talk like that, after all he's done for us.

LEFT F. An' wot's 'e done fer us, I'd like ter know? Works us daown ter ther bone without so much as Thank You. And fer wot, I arsks yer? Fer wot? Chysin' abaht after some bloke wot's been dead fer years. A lot I care whether the Boss finds 'im. I 'aven't seen the inside of a carpet slipper fer weeks. Wot wouldn't I give fer a bath? Cor! I don't 'alf whistle!

RIGHT F. Yes, the odour *is* unpleasant, certainly. Especially to feet like us, who've always been brought up to regard cleanliness as next to godliness. . . . Still, I must say, I don't see that grumbling does much good. And, look here, old chap, I do wish you wouldn't speak of the Master in that way. It makes such a bad impression when other people are about. Of course, I know you and I know quite well you don't mean a word of it. . . .

LEFT F. Don't I, jest? That's all you knows! Look 'ere, wot'd you and yer precious Boss do if I was ter tell yer I wasn't goin' a step further? You'd 'ave ter carry me! 'Ow'd yer like that, eh?

RIGHT F. [*coldly*]. Of course, you're perfectly entitled to act as you think best. We can't stop you. I might just as well take the same attitude myself. . . . It's

113

a matter of loyalty: either one appreciates that kind of thing, or one doesn't.

Left F. You and yer Public School edjerkytion! Ort ter 'ave bin a sky pilot, you ort!

Right F. It's very easy to sneer. But the fact remains that without some kind of standards a fellow just goes to pieces. One saw enough of that in the War. Who were the best officers? The boys who had been captains of their school fifteens. And the more one knocks about the world, the more one comes to realise. . . .

Left F. Ow, lay orf it! Yer mikes me sick! I ain't goin' ter listen ter another of yer lectures on the Team Spirit, an' that's stryte!

Right F. Sorry, old chap. I didn't mean to jaw. Let's change the subject, shall we? . . . You said just now that Sir Francis Crewe was dead. Well, I'm sure he's not. . . . And what's more, I'm on his track at last!

Left F. Go on! You're kiddin'.

Right F. Oh no, I'm not. I'll prove it to you. I've been working on the case for months, now: I didn't want to say anything till I'd got it watertight. . . . And it's all so beautifully simple, really. . . . Do you know what gave me the first clue?

Left F. Wot?

Right F. I happened to notice, one morning, that the Master's brown shoes had a little indentation on either side of the toe-cap, about half an inch long. At the time, I thought no more about it: It wasn't till the other day, fitting the facts together and try-ing them this way and that, that the whole thing flashed upon me. Do you know what had made those marks? [*Dramatically*.] Roller-skates!

LEFT F. But wot's that got ter do with Sir Francis Crewe?

RIGHT F. I'll give you all the stages of my reasoning later: But it was really those skate-marks which led me to his hiding-place.

LEFT F. Yer means you've seen 'im?

RIGHT F. Oh no. I've never seen him yet. How could I? The Master never lets us go out alone.

LEFT F. But yer knows where 'e is?

RIGHT F. I do.

LEFT F. Go on then, spit it aht!

RIGHT F. [*impressively*]. At this very moment, Sir Francis Crewe is . . . [*glances round him*]. No. Better not tell you here. There may be spies about. Come behind the milestone.

[*The* FEET *disappear*.]

TWO CHORUS LEADERS.

> Now through night's caressing grip
> Earth and all her oceans slip,
> Capes of China slide away
> From her fingers into day
> And the Americas incline
> Coasts towards her shadow line.
> Now the ragged vagrants creep
> Into crooked holes to sleep:
> Just and unjust, worst and best,
> Change their places as they rest:

115

Awkward lovers lie in fields
Where disdainful beauty yields:
While the splendid and the proud
Naked stand before the crowd
And the losing gambler gains
And the beggar entertains:
May sleep's healing power extend
Through these hours to our friend.
Unpursued by hostile force,
Traction engine, bull or horse
Or revolting succubus;
Calmly till the morning break
Let him lie, then gently wake.

CURTAIN

ACT III
CHORUS

A man and a dog are entering a city: They are approach-
    ing a centre of culture:
First the suburban dormitories spreading over fields,
Villas on vegetation like saxifrage on stone,
Isolated from each other like cases of fever
And uniform in design, uniform as nurses.
To each a lean-to shed, containing a well-oiled engine of
    escape.
Section these dwellings: expose the life of a people
Living by law and the length of a reference,
See love in its disguises and the losses of the heart,
Cats and old silver inspire heroic virtues
And psychic fields, accidentally generated, destroy
    whole families.
Extraordinary tasks are set: a ploughman's hand ac-
    quires the most exquisite calligraphy,
A scheme is prepared for draining the North Sea, with
    the aid of books from the local library:
One has a vision in the bathroom after a family quarrel:
    he kneels on the cork mat:
A naturalist leaves in a cab in time for the breaking of
    the meres.

A youth with boils lies face down in bed, his mother over
    him;
Tenderly she squeezes from his trembling body the last
    dregs of his childhood.

Writer, be glib: please them with scenes of theatrical
    bliss and horror,
Whose own slight gestures tell their doom with a subtle-
    ty quite foreign to the stage.
For who dare patiently tell, tell of their sorrow
Without let or variation of season, streaming up in par-
    allel from the little houses
And unabsorbed by their ironic treasures
Exerts on the rigid dome of the unpierced sky its enor-
    mous pressures?

But look: While we were talking, they have not stood
    still,
They have passed up the parade, the site of shops:
Goods are displayed: behind plate glass
One satin slipper austerely arranged
On an inky background of blackest velvet:
A waxen sandboy in skiing kit
Dumb and violet among vapour lamps.
High in the air, in empty space,
Five times a minute a mug is filled
And in ten-foot letters, time after time,
Words are spelt out and wiped away.
He moves amazed among the well-fed multitudes;
They glance at the stranger with the glance of those

Who have paid their allowance to be left alone.
And now they reach the Nineveh Hotel;
Consider this hotel: its appointments and fittings:
Five hundred bedrooms, with h and c, —
Three hundred bathrooms: 375 W.Cs.:
Inspect the dining-hall: seating 2000:
The waiters scuttling from side to side
Like goldfish feeding the valuable people:
Admire the shining silver and cutlery
Stamped with the mark of that sombre town
Which fouls the Don still fresh from the moor
And the beautiful glassware blown on the Danube:
And stand in the vestibule spacious and gilded
As our hero enters to sign his name.
Old men afraid of reflections in glass
Are ushering ladies out to their cars,
Veiled and valued, through revolving doors.
Paid to be pretty, pumped into cloth,
Ranked by pillars pages wait,
At signals, like gulls from a nesting stack,
To rise on their toes and tear away.

Come in:

SCENE I

[*The vestibule of the Nineveh Hotel.* PORTER. PAGES. *Enter* ALAN *and* DOG.]

PORTER. I'm glad you've come, sir.
         You want a room, sir?

ALAN.   Please.

PORTER. I'm sorry to be a trouble, sir:
         A single or a double, sir?

ALAN.   A single, please.

PORTER. I'm still in doubt, sir.
         With bathroom or without, sir?

ALAN.   With bathroom, please.

PORTER. Just sign your name, sir.
         And date the same, sir.
         Here, quickly, page boy,
         Or you'll put me in a rage, boy.
         Show this gentleman up to
         Room 132.

PAGE.   Let me take your bag, sir.
         It'll save you fag, sir.
         Please follow me, sir.
         I've got the key, sir.

CHORUS. Make way, make way:

120

This gentleman has come to stay.
He wants a room where he may rest,
But not the best, but not the best:
He's only a provincial guest.

PORTER [*sees* DOG]. I'm sorry, dogs are not allowed, sir,
I didn't see him in the crowd, sir.

ALAN. But that's absurd, my dog and I
Are never parted: tell me why,
If not I'll give you back my keys
And leave this moment, if you please!

[*Enter the* TWO JOURNALISTS. *The* 2ND
JOURNALIST *is very drunk.*]

2ND JOURNALIST [*singing*].
The bluebells bloomed on the Baltic shore
When Kit was Schneider-Creusot's love.

1ST J. Why look, there's Alan!

2ND J.   My dear old boy!
To see you once more is indeed a joy!

[2ND J. *throws his arms round* ALAN'S *neck.*]

1ST J. He means no evil
But he's tight as the devil.

ALAN. I always hoped we should meet again.

1ST J. What about your search? Has it been in
vain?

ALAN. He never left England at all, it appears.

2ND J. [*who has wandered off into a corner, sings*].
Alice is gone and I'm alone,
Nobody understands
How lovely were her Fire Alarms,
How fair her German Bands!

121

1st J. [*to* 2nd J.]. Stop! Stop! You make
              My stomach ache!

                            [*To* ALAN.]

              Are you staying here?

ALAN.   I'd hoped to. But they won't allow the dog.

1st J.   They won't?
              I'll settle that: You see if I don't!
              Porter!

PORTER. What can I do, sir?
              To satisfy you, sir?

                [1st J. *whispers something in his ear.*]

PORTER. O O Sir,
              I didn't know, sir!

                            [*To* ALAN.]

              I'm so sorry, sir.
              I made a mistake, sir.
              I was in a hurry, sir.
              Don't worry, sir.
              Of course we'll take, sir,
              Your dog too, sir,
              As well as you, sir.

                            [*To* PAGE.]

              This dog you must take, boy,
              And feed on cake, boy.

                [*Exeunt* PORTER, PAGE *and* DOG.]

ALAN.   Whatever did you say?

1st J.   Ah, that's a secret I can't give away!
              Let's come and eat.

      [*They go out.* 2nd J. *lingering behind, sings,
      out of tune and with great pathos.*]

2ND J. [*singing*]. O how I cried when Alice died
      The day we were to have wed!
      We never had our Roasted Duck
      And now she's a Loaf of Bread!

                      [*He staggers out.*]

CURTAIN

SCENE II

[*The restaurant of the Nineveh Hotel. In the foreground are tables with diners: including* ALAN *and the* TWO JOURNALISTS. *In the background is a small stage for cabaret. The entire setting of this scene should convey an impression of brutal, noisy vulgarity and tasteless extravagance. Band music.*]

VOICES.   And as for her hat, my dear . . .

Le Touquet was lousy this year.

Have you read *The Virgin Policeman*?

Yes we did. We got right to the Docks.

There's his new one.

There were lots of children without any socks.

You mean the blue one?

It was divine. We found a dive.

I'm flying next week to the Bahamas.

And danced with the sailors. I felt so *alive*.

What I say is: damn a man with holes in his
pyjamas!

Darling, you look wonderful tonight!

One of those schools one has never heard of.

CABARET ANNOUNCER. Ladies and Gentlemen! The
romance of foreign lands has been celebrated by

every song-writer. But we feel that insufficient justice has been done to our own country. We are presenting therefore to you tonight Madame Bubbi, in a new song entitled: *Rhondda Moon*. When you have heard her, I'm sure you will be convinced, as we are, that, in the opportunities which she offers to the Tender Passion, Britain is second to none! Madame Bubbi!

> [*Enter* MADAME BUBBI, *an immense woman in a sequin dress.*]

M. B. [*sings*].

I come with a message to the farmers and the cities;
I've a simple slogan, it's just: Love British!
British Romance, British joys,
British chorus girls and chorus boys.

The Sahara makes hearts go pit-a-pat,
Glamorganshire can do better than that!
Wherever you go, be it east or west,
Remember British Love is quite the best.

People sing songs about Tennessee
But foreign men won't do for me.
I don't want a dago, I don't want a Greek,
I've got what I want and that's a British Sheik.

CHORUS. On the Rhondda
My time I squander
Watching for my miner boy:
He may be rough and tough
But he surely is hot stuff
And he's slender, to-me-tender,

He's my only joy:
Lovers' meeting,
Lovers' greeting,
O his arms will be around me soon!
For I am growing fonder
Out yonder as I wander
And I ponder 'neath a Rhondda moon!

VOICES OF DINERS. I bought five yards.

I always use Corps de Femme myself.

He's in the Guards.

Oh, she's already on the shelf.

I told him I couldn't do without it.

Have you read *The Virgin Policeman*?

The customs officer was perfectly sweet about it.

> [*Enter the* NINEVEH GIRLS. *All that is mechanical, shallow, silly, hideous and unbearably tragic in the antics of a modern cabaret chorus should be expressed here in its most exaggerated form. Crude lighting. Rowdy music.*]

NINEVEH GIRLS [*sing*].

We are girls of different ages,
All sorts of girls at all sorts of stages, we've
Come to delight you,
Come to excite you,
Come to present our revue!
Fair girls, dear girls,
Dark girls, stark girls,
Glad girls, bad girls,
Poor girls, we've-met-before-girls, we
All would welcome you.

Desires, ambitions, anxieties fill us,
We come from brick rectories and sham-Tudor villas,
    It's our profession
    To cure your depression
    And banish those melancholy blues.
Old girls, bold girls,
Shy girls, fly girls,
Kiss-girls, sis-girls,
Lean girls, do-you-get-what-I-mean-girls, you
    Only have to choose.

We lift our legs for your masculine inspection,
You can admire us without our correction, we
    Do this nightly,
    We hope we're not unsightly
    Or all our labours are vain!
Neat girls, sweet girls,
Gym girls, slim girls,
Meek girls, technique girls,
Pat girls, com-up-to-my-flat-girls, we
    Hope to see you again!
        [*Applause. A solitary* DINER *with an eye-glass*
        beckons the WAITER.]

DINER.   Waiter!
WAITER. At once, sir!
        You want, sir?
DINER.   Bring me the third girl from the right.
        [*The* WAITER *blows a signal on his whistle and*
        the chosen girl comes down from the stage. The
        WAITER *catches her head under his arm as*

though she were a fowl and holds her so that the
DINER *can pinch her thigh. The girl does not*
offer the least resistance.]

WAITER. Will she do, sir?

Or will you choose anew, sir?

DINER. No. I'll have this one.

WAITER. Will you have her roast, sir,

Or on Japanese Toast, sir?

With Sauce Allemagne, sir,

Or stewed in white wine, sir?

DINER. Stewed, I think. But I'll have the finger-nails
served separately as a savoury. Oh, and don't for-
get to remind the Chef to stir the pot with a sprig of
rosemary. It makes all the difference.

[WAITER *bows and retires, carrying the girl over
his shoulder.*]

CABARET ANNOUNCER. Our next item is Destructive
Desmond!

[*Deafening applause.* DESTRUCTIVE DES-
MOND *comes on to the stage, followed by atten-
dants carrying a large oil painting.* DESMOND
*is dressed as a schoolboy, with ink-stains on
his cheeks, a crumpled eton collar, a striped
cap, broken bootlaces, dishevelled stockings and
shorts. He is a stocky, middle-aged man, with
an inflamed, pugnacious face and very hairy
knees.*]

ONE OF THE DINERS TO ANOTHER. Haven't you seen
him before? Oh, he's marvellous! I saw him last
winter in New York. He burnt an entire first folio

Shakespeare, page by page. I've never laughed so much in all my life.

DESMOND. Hullo, fellows! Here we are again! Has anyone got a nice old poetry-book for me to read? I do love a bit of poetry! [*Loud laughter from the audience.*] You haven't? Never mind! This evening, I've got a real treat for you. But, first of all, is there any gentleman in the audience who knows anything about painting? no, not painting the greenhouse. [*Laughter.*] Pictures! Come on, don't be shy. Thank you, sir. Will you step up on the stage a moment?

[*An ART EXPERT, a nice, rather ineffective man in pince-nez, comes up. He is evidently a bona-fide member of the audience and not in the conspiracy. He does not at first understand what is going to happen.*]

DESMOND [*winking at the audience*]. So you're an Art expert, sir?

ART EXPERT. Well, er, without wishing to be immodest, I think I have some claim to that title, yes. I am the curator of the gallery at Barchester.

DESMOND. Excellent! Just the man I wanted to meet! You see, sir, I wanted to ask your advice about a picture I've just bought. Would you care to look at it?

A. E. [*adjusting his pince-nez*]. Certainly, certainly. If I can be of any service....

[DESMOND *signs to the attendants to uncover the picture. The* ART EXPERT *bends down to examine it. After a moment, he utters an exclama-*

tion, takes a magnifying glass from his pocket and studies every inch of the canvas with great care. The audience titters with delight: everybody else in the room seems to know exactly what will happen.]

A. E. [*standing up, evidently very much excited*]. Do you know, Mr, er Desmond . . . it's a very remarkable thing, very remarkable indeed . . . this picture is a Rembrandt!

DESMOND. Are you sure of that?

A. E. Quite positive. There can be no doubt whatever.

DESMOND [*playing always to the audience, and mimicking the over-cultured tones of the* ART EXPERT]. No doubt whatever? Fancy that, now! And will you be so kind as to tell these ladies and gentlemen how much this Rembrandt of mine is worth?

A. E. Oh, speaking offhand, I should say about sixty thousand pounds.

DESMOND [*as before*]. Isn't that a lot of money! Dear, Oh dear! And suppose something were to *happen* to my beautiful picture [*unseen by the* ART EXPERT, *but visible to the audience, he produces an enormous penknife: the audience are delighted*] do you think Mr Rembrandt would paint me another one like it?

A. E. [*smiling*]. No, he couldn't, I'm afraid. He's dead.

DESMOND. Oh, he's dead, is he? I *am* sorry! I must send some flowers. What did he die of?

[*The* ART EXPERT *doesn't quite know what to make of this fooling. He has become aware of the curiously hostile mood of* DESMOND *and the*

130

audience towards himself. He stands there awkwardly, smiling but uneasy.]

DESMOND. Well, well [*he flourishes the knife*] if Mr Rembrandt's dead, he won't be angry with me: that's one comfort. And anyhow, I suppose I can do what I like with my own picture. . . .

A. E. [*suddenly realising what* DESMOND *is going to do*]. Mr Desmond! . . . You're not going to . . . ?

DESMOND. Not going to what?

A. E. [*gasping*]. To . . . destroy this picture?

DESMOND [*now openly sneering at him*]. And why shouldn't I destroy it, may I ask? Isn't it mine?

A. E. . . . Yes, er, of course. . . . But I mean. . . . You *can't*. . . . it's a masterpiece!

DESMOND. Oh, it's a masterpiece, is it? And how would you define a masterpiece, Mr Art Expert?

A. E. Something unique . . . a work of genius . . . which can't be replaced . . . priceless . . . [*he stammers, amidst the merriment of the audience, and cannot go on*].

DESMOND [*signs to the attendants to uncover a second picture*]. Is *this* a masterpiece?

A. E. [*contemptuously*]. No, most certainly not!

DESMOND. Why isn't it?

A. E. In the first place because it's a completely tasteless piece of third-rate Victorian landscape painting of which you'll find examples in every boardinghouse in England: And secondly, because it isn't even an original. You could get as many copies as you wanted from the publishers for a shilling a piece.

DESMOND. Well, all I can say is: I think it's a very nice
picture. I like it much better than Mr Rembrandt's,
which you say is so valuable. [*Pointing to the Rembrandt.*] Why, this is all *brown*! More like a chest of
drawers! Ugh, how I hate you!

[*Raises knife to slash the Rembrandt canvas.*]

A. E. [*almost in tears*]. Stop! I protest against this disgraceful exhibition! I appeal to the ladies and
gentlemen of the audience. Surely you won't allow
this to go on?

DESMOND. Aha! So you appeal to the audience, do you?
Very well! [*To the audience.*] Ladies and gentlemen,
I leave it entirely in your hands: which picture
would you rather see cut to bits, this landscape
which Mr Expert so much despises, or old mahogany Rembrandt?

ALL THE DINERS.

Rembrandt! Rembrandt!

DESMOND [*brutally, to* ART EXPERT]. You hear what
they say? And now, get off my platform? If you
don't like it, you can do the other thing!

A. E. [*putting his hands to his head*]. Either these people
are mad, or I am! [*He jumps down from the stage and
runs out of the restaurant.*]

[DESMOND *waves an ironic goodbye after him.
The drums begin to roll. The audience groan with
delight.* DESMOND, *standing before the Rembrandt, works himself up into a state of hysterical
fury. He makes faces at the canvas, shows his
teeth, shakes his fist, spits.*]

132

DESMOND [*as the drums reach their climax*]. Grrrr! Take
that, you brute! [*slashes canvas with his knife*]
and that! and that!

> [*Finale of trumpets. The attendants hold up the
> slashed picture and* DESMOND *puts his arm
> through it several times. Then he strikes it
> from their hands and tramples on it on the
> floor. Terrific applause.* DESMOND *bows and
> exit.*]

> > [*A trumpet.*]

A VOICE.

> Here comes Miss Lou Vipond,
> The star of whom the world is fond!
> [*All the diners jump up and rush towards the
> entrance, to get a peep.* ALAN *is one of the first.
> As* MISS VIPOND *passes across the stage, she is
> completely hidden by the crowd.*]

1ST JOURNALIST.

> Alan, old boy, come back! come back!
> Don't you cross that harpy's track!

2ND J.   If you fall for that dame, it'll be your undoing:
> She's brought enough good men to their
> ruin.

ALAN [*who is standing on a table in order to see better*].

> You fellows talk the most utter rot!
> All other women can go to pot!
> I'm true to Iris.

> > [*He catches sight of* MISS VIPOND.]
> > By Jove, she's a stunner!
> What a face! I'm dazzled!

133

[*He jumps down from his table into the middle of the crowd.*]

1ST J. [*covering his eyes*]. The kid's a gonner!

VOICES FROM THE CROWD ROUND ALAN.

    She's stopped to speak to a stranger!

    Then he's in danger!

    Look at her eyes!

    What a lovely surprise!

    She pretends she feels tired!

    O she's inspired!

    She leans on his arm!

    She knows her charm!

    She's going to speak!

    It makes his knees weak!

    She has asked him to visit her room!

    He goes to his doom!

[ALAN, *his face transformed by joy, breaks through the crowd and rushes forward.*]

ALAN [*to* JOURNALISTS].

    Where can I get some flowers

    So long after hours?

      [*Without waiting for an answer, he runs out.*]

CHORUS.

    Inform the Press, inform the Press,

    Miss Vipond's had one more success!

    It's in the air, it's in the air,

    She's going to have a new affair!

    Make way, make way,

    This gentleman has come to stay!

He wants the best, he wants the best,
He's more than a provincial guest!

He quickly fell, he quickly fell,
He lost his heart in our hotel!
He's going to start, he's going to start,
He's starting now to break his heart!

CURTAIN

SCENE III

[*Before the curtain. Enter simultaneously* ALAN (*left*) *and the* DOG (*right*). *They meet in the middle of the stage.* ALAN *is in tails. He carries an immense bouquet of flowers.*]

ALAN [*in a great hurry*]. Hullo, Doggy! How's life? [*The* DOG *fawns on him.*] Not now, there's a good dog! I'm in an awful hurry. Just think, in another minute I shall be with her! I believe, if I didn't see her again, I should go crazy! But you can't understand that, can you, Doggy? As long as you get your food and a nice warm mat to lie on, you're perfectly happy. I wish I were a dog! No, I'm damn glad I'm not! [*He pats the* DOG'S *head absentmindedly.*] Well, I must be off. [*The* DOG *puts its paws on* ALAN'S *shoulders.*] Here, I say! That's enough! Let me alone, can't you? What's the matter with you this evening? Down, sir! [*He pushes the* DOG *roughly aside.*] Now you've made my coat dirty. I shall have to get it brushed. Silly fool! [*He takes a step forward. Immediately, the* DOG *jumps up and drags the flowers from his hand, scattering them in all directions.*] Francis, how dare you! You

clumsy brute! [ALAN *gives the* DOG *a kick.*] Get
out! [*The* DOG *does not move. There is a pause.*] I
say, Francis, old boy, I didn't mean to do that!
Honestly I didn't! I've never kicked you before,
have I? You just made me angry with you for the
moment. I'm sorry. . . . Why do you look at me like
that? You can't pretend I really hurt you: Now,
can you? Let me see. . . . [*He moves his hand to-
wards the* DOG. *The* DOG *retreats a little.*] Oh,very
well, if you'd rather not. Here: Shake a paw! [*The*
DOG *does not move.*] All right, then: sulk if you
want to. I've said I'm sorry. I can't do any more,
can I? And anyhow, it was all your fault. [*Pointing
to the flowers.*] Just look at them: all ruined! Now I
shall have to get some more, and they cost five
shillings each. What made you do it, Francis? Ha
ha ha! I believe you're jealous again! Was that why?
Well, you are a queer dog! But you wait till you see
her, Francis. She's the most marvellous creature in
the world! Goodness knows what she can see in a
chap like me! Her eyes, why, you've no idea. . . .
[*But the* DOG *has turned and, with great dignity,
slowly walked off the stage.*] He's gone! Funny! I ex-
pect he'll be all right tomorrow. . . . And now!
[ALAN *straightens his coat and smooths his hair.*] I
must get those flowers. [*Looks at his watch.*] Good
God! I'm five seconds late already!

[He rushes out].

SCENE IV

[*The Nineveh Hotel. The stage is divided in half. The right-hand scene represents* MISS VIPOND'S *bedroom. The left-hand scene is the corridor outside it. When the curtain rises, the bedroom is in darkness. The corridor is illuminated. The* DOG *is sitting on a chest outside the bedroom door. A grandfather clock stands in the corner. Enter the* MANAGER, *with a chorus of* WAITERS, PAGES *and* CHAMBERMAIDS.]

MANAGER. When he gets his bill tomorrow
          What will Mr Norman say?
        Will he shoot himself for sorrow
          All on a summer's day?

CHORUS. Perhaps he'll only lose his mind,
        Go wild and feed among the lilies:
      Tell us, if you'd be so kind,
         . Tell us what the bill is.

MANAGER. 20 cases of champagne,
        A finest pedigree Great Dane,
        Half a dozen Paris frocks,
        A sable fur, a silver fox,
        Bottles of scent and beauty salves,
        An MG Midget with overhead valves,

1 doz pairs of shoes and boots,
6 lounge, 1 tails and 3 dress suits,
A handsome two-piece bathing-dress,
An electric razor, a trouser-press,
A cutter for cigars, two lighters,
10 autographs of famous writers,
Berths and tickets in advance
For a trip round Southern France:
Add to this his bed and board.

CHORUS. It's more than one man can afford.

MANAGER. This we'll keep until the morning.
Remember, do not give him warning.

[*Exit.*]
[*Song and Step Dance.*]

WAITERS. If we're late
Or break a plate
He won't be rude.
If we served him nude
Would he know?
No No No!
He's in love!

PAGES. If we lose
All his shoes,
Say Go to Hell
When he rings the bell,
He won't know:
No No No!
He's in love!

CHAMBERMAID. If I stops
Emptying the slops,

139

Leaves a dead
Mouse in the bed,
He won't know:
No No No,
He's in love!

[*A bell rings. The* CHORUS *arrange themselves under the* HEAD WAITER.]

HEAD WAITER.

The Nineveh Hotel holds the copyright
Of the Epithalamium we are going to recite.

CHORUS [*reciting, with a background of eighteenth-century music*].

You who return tonight to a narrow bed
With one name running sorrowfully through your
sorrowful head,
You who have never been touched, and you, pale
lover,
Who left the house this morning kissed all over,
You little boys also of quite fourteen
Beginning to realise just what we mean,
Fill up glasses with champagne and drink again.

It's not a new school or factory to which we summon,
We're here today because of a man and a woman.
Oh Chef, employ your continental arts
To celebrate the union of two loving hearts!
Waiters, be deft, and slip, you pages, by
To honour the god to name whom is to lie:
Fill up glasses with champagne and drink again.

[*The corridor begins to darken.*]

140

Already he has brought the swallows past the
    Scillies
To chase each other skimming under English bridges,
Has loosed the urgent pollen on the glittering coun-
    try
To find the pistil, force its burglar's entry,
He moves us also and up the marble stair
He leads the figures matched in beauty and desire:
Fill up glasses with champagne and drink again.

        [*The corridor is now completely dark.* MISS VI-
        POND'S *bedroom is illuminated.* ALAN *stands*
        embracing MISS VIPOND, *who is a shopwindow*
        dummy, very beautifully dressed. When the
        dummy is to speak, ALAN *runs behind it and*
        speaks in falsetto.]

ALAN.

My swan, so beautiful to my five senses,
When I look on you, in a moment I lose my de-
    fences,
My clumsy heart forgets herself and dances.

DUMMY.

O lion, O sun, encompass me with power,
Feed lion, shine sun, for in your glory I flower,
Create the huge and gorgeous summer in an hour.

VOICES OF WAITERS' CHORUS [*outside in the corridor*].

What would you give that she might live?

ALAN.

I would give the Netherlands with all their canals,
The earth of the Ukraine, the Niagara Falls,
The Eiffel Tower also and the Dome of St Paul's.

141

CHORUS OUTSIDE.

What would you do to keep her true?

ALAN.

I would hunt the enormous whale in the Arctic lowlands,

I would count all the starlings in the British Islands,

I would run through fighting Europe in absolute silence.

DUMMY.

But men are treacherous, I know, as the North-East wind,

They speak of loving but another is in their mind,

And you will leave me tomorrow morning for another find.

ALAN.

True, there was one I thought I loved beyond measure.

Here is her picture, I destroy it to give you pleasure.

For, love, in your arms I find the only treasure.

[*He tears up the photograph of* IRIS *and scatters the pieces at the dummy's feet.*]

DUMMY.

Our sails are set. O launch upon love's ocean,

Fear has no means there of locomotion

And death cannot exhaust us with his endless devotion.

[ALAN *begins to embrace and undress the dummy. The bedroom slowly darkens. From the complete darkness of the corridor, the voices of the*

WAITERS' CHORUS *are heard, gradually receding.*]

CHORUS.

It's not only this we praise, it's the general love:
Let cat's mew rise to a scream on the tool-shed roof,
Let son come home tonight to his anxious mother,
Let the vicar lead the choirboy into a dark corner.
The orchard shall flower tonight that flowers every
    hundred years,
The boots and the slavey be found dutch-kissing on
    the stairs:
Fill up glasses with champagne and drink again.

Let this be kept as a generous hour by all,
This once let the uncle settle his nephew's bill,
Let the nervous lady's table gaucheness be forgiven,
Let the thief's explanation of the theft be taken,
The boy caught smoking shall escape the usual whip-
    ping,
Tonight the expensive whore shall give herself for
    nothing:
Fill up glasses with champagne and drink again.

The landlocked state shall get its port today,
The midnight worker in the laboratory by the sea
Shall discover under the cross-wires that which he
    looks for,
Tonight the asthmatic clerk shall dream he's a boxer,
Let the cold heart's wish be granted, the desire for a
    desire,

O give to the coward now his hour of power:
Fill up glasses with champagne and drink again.

> [*The bedroom is now completely dark. In the cor-
> ridor, spotlights suddenly illuminate the chest
> and the grandfather clock. Beside the chest the*
> DOG *is lying with its paws crossed.*]

DOG'S SKIN. Ticker! Ticker! Are you awake? [*The
Clock strikes one.*] It's only me, the dog's skin that
hides that eccentric young man. I hope you admire
my accent? I've lived so long with them, I have all
the émigré's pride, at having forgotten my own.
I'm quite déraciné, as they say in Bloomsbury.
When I first paid them a visit, before I gave up my
nationality and was still an Irish Wolfhound, I was
very romantic. The odour of a particular arm-chair,
the touch of certain fingers, excited me to rash
generalisations which I believed to be profound. I
composed poems that I imagined highly idiomatic,
on the words 'walk' and 'dinner'. And it was in
this romantic mood that I decided to throw in my
lot with theirs and sever all ties with my past. My
dearest ambition was to be accepted naturally as one
of them. I was soon disillusioned! To them I was
only a skin, valued for its associations with that
very life I had hoped to abandon. Small children
misunderstood by their parents rubbed tearful
cheeks against me and whispered secrets to their
doggie. I ask you . . . Doggie! Young men wore me
at charades to arouse in others undisguised human
amusement and desire. Talking about charades,

Ticker, are you interested in literature at all? [*The Clock strikes two*.] You are? So am I.

In the old days, before I became a skin, I used to be the pet of a very famous author. He talked all day to yours truly. He suffered terribly from indigestion, poor fellow, and wrote what was called 'virile' poetry. He was knighted for it during the war. Well, I'll tell you a story about him. One night (it was nearly one o'clock in the morning, as a matter of fact) he was pretty tight on whisky and we had a real heart-to-heart. George, he says (I was called George in those days), George, he says, come here. I came, rather crossly, to tell you the truth, I was sleepy and wishing he'd go to bed. George, look at me. Do I make you sick? (By the way, I forgot to tell you that it was during the war, at the time of the big German offensive in March of 18). Less than a hundred miles from here, young men are being blown to pieces. Listen, you can hear the guns doing it. (It was quite true, you could. We lived on the South Downs and it was a still night.) Every time I hear that, I say to myself: You fired that shell. It isn't the cold general on his white horse, nor the owner of the huge factory, nor the luckless poor, but you. Yes, I and those like me. Invalid poets with a fountain pen, undersized professors in a classroom, we, the sedentary and learned, whose schooling cost the most, the least conspicuous of them all, are the assassins. (I'm giving you his own words. Whisky always made him a bit rhetorical.) We have conjured up all the vigours and all the splendours, skilfully transferred our envy into an image of the universal mother, for which the lad of seventeen whom we have always sent and will send again against our terrors, gladly immolates himself. Men are falling through the air in flames and choking slowly in the dark recesses of the sea to assuage our pride. Our pride! Who cannot work without incessant cups of tea, spend whole days weeping in our rooms, immoderately desire little girls on beaches and buy them sweets, cannot pass a mirror without staring, for whom a slight cold is enough to create a day-dream of our death-bed with appropriate organ-music. . . . Now wasn't that queer? It was the last talk I ever had with him. He couldn't bear the sight of me after that evening and sold me as soon as he could.

Just like a man! You know, Ticker, I think the important thing to remember about Man is that pictures mean more to him than people. Take sex, for instance. Well, you've seen what it was like this evening. Sometimes it's funny and sometimes it's sad, but it's always hanging about like a smell of drains. Too many ideas in their heads! To them I'm an idea, you're an idea, everything's an idea. That's why we're here. Funny thing, Ticker, that we should both be in the same play. They can't do without us. If it wasn't for me, this young man of mine would never be able to get a good night's rest: and if it wasn't for you he'd never wake up. And look what we do to the audience! When I come on, they start sighing, thinking of spring, meadows and goodness knows what else: While you make them demand a tragic ending, with you they associate an immensely complicated system of awards and punishments.

[*During this speech, the corridor has been gradually illuminated.*]

Heavens. it's getting light and you've forgotten to strike! Hurry up! [*The Clock strikes six.*] I think someone's coming and my lodger is waking up. So long! Abyssinia.

[*The* DOG *stretches.* FRANCIS CREWE *gets out of the skin, lays it on the chest, looks cautiously round and tip-toes out.*]

[MANAGER, WAITERS, PAGES, *etc. enter singing (Air: John Peel)*].

MANAGER.

The sun has risen and it shines through the blind,
This lover must awaken and recall to mind
Though the pillow be soft and the lady be kind,
Yet the man has to pay in the morning.

CHORUS. For in Nineveh Hotel the most humble guest,
Be he old, be he young, he may take a good rest,
He may smoke cigars, he may order the best,
But we hand him the bill in the morning.

[*The* MANAGER *knocks loudly at the bedroom door.* ALAN *appears in pyjamas.*]

ALAN. What's all this row,
I can't see you now?

147

CHORUS. We're sorry, sir,
To be a worry, sir,
But we're in a hurry, sir.
We want our money, sir.
Here is our bill, sir.

[*They give him the bill. Pause.*]

Oh, don't be ill, sir!

ALAN. Fifteen hundred! It's absurd!
This will have to be deferred.
I'm sorry, gentlemen, to say
Just at this moment I cannot pay.
You shall have your money another day.

CHORUS. Till we have our due, we stay.

ALAN. Here's a to-do!
I must borrow from Lou.

[*He speaks into the bedroom, which is in darkness.*]

Darling, I'm sorry to be such a bother
But some stupid tradesman is making a
pother
(It's nothing really) about my account:
So will you lend it me, darling Lou?
Fifteen hundred pounds will do.

[*No answer.*]

Darling, please,
Don't be a tease,
They're waiting here,
They will fetch the Police.
Please be a dear!

[*No answer.*]

148

Say something, do!
I want help, Lou!

[*No answer.*]

Why don't you answer?
I tell you, I'm in danger!

[*No answer.*]

Last night you spoke.
This is no joke!

[*No answer.*]

What is the matter, what have I done?
Last night you called me your lion and your
sun.
Speak to me, please, just one little word,
I don't understand you! Oh, this is absurd!

[*A pause.*]

I am your lover!
Don't say that's over!
That can't be what you mean!

[*A pause.*]

I won't believe it!

[*A pause.*]

All right, I'll leave it.
Oh, I'm in hell!

[*He turns to the* MANAGER *and others outside
in the corridor.*]

MANAGER. Well?
ALAN. Gentlemen, what can I say?
I cannot pay!
MANAGER. This is a most regrettable occasion.
I must go at once to the police station.
Alphonse.

ALPHONSE. Yes sah?

MANAGER. Tell the Porter he's not to let
This man go out: and don't forget!
[*Exeunt* MANAGER *and others.*]

ALAN. Lou! Lou!
There is only one thing left to do,
Something that the Romans knew,
In a bath I'll open a vein
And end my life with little pain.
I'll go at once and turn
The water on and then return
For the razor to relieve
Me for ever of my grief.

[*He enters the darkened bedroom and disappears.*
FRANCIS CREWE *comes into the corridor, takes
the skin from the chest and hastily begins getting
into it. While he is doing so,* ALAN *reappears at
the bedroom door.*]

ALAN. What are you doing to my dog? You've killed
him? Oh, this is the end of everything!

FRANCIS. Alan!

ALAN. You know my name? Who are you? What do
you want?

FRANCIS. I ought to know your name by this time.
I've been with you long enough.

ALAN. My Goodness! You don't mean . . . ?

FRANCIS. Yes, I'm your faithful doggy. This is how I
look in mufti. But you can go on calling me Francis.
It's my real name.

ALAN. My God, who are you? You're not . . . ?

150

FRANCIS [*mimicking* ALAN'S *voice*].

> 'Is the name Sir Francis Crewe,
>
> English, known perhaps to you?'

ALAN. Francis! At last! [*They embrace.*] Oh, this is the happiest moment of my life! Everything's all right now!

FRANCIS. I'm glad you think so.

ALAN. Well, isn't it?

FRANCIS [*nodding towards the bedroom door*]. What about Miss Vipond?

ALAN. Oh, that's all over. I was mad, I think. She's the most utter bitch.

FRANCIS. I could have told you that.

ALAN [*laughing*]. You did try to, didn't you? I say, Francis, I'm most awfully sorry I kicked you.

FRANCIS. That's all right. It was my fault, really. My attempts at dissuasion were somewhat crude. You've no idea what self-control it took not to answer you back, though. You'd have got a shock if the dog had spoken!

ALAN. Yes, shouldn't I? . . . I say, Francis, there's so much I want to ask you, I don't know where to begin! Whatever made you dress up as a dog, at all?

FRANCIS. I'll tell you all about that, but not now. The first question is, what are we going to do?

ALAN. Well . . . go back to Pressan Ambo, of course.

FRANCIS. You really want to?

ALAN. Of course I want to.

FRANCIS. And marry my charming sister?

ALAN. Yes . . . rather!

FRANCIS. You don't sound quite so enthusiastic as you were. Still, a promise is a promise, isn't it? Let's hope it won't be broken. . . . You're longing to be back in Pressan again, I suppose? You know, you may find it rather changed.

ALAN. Rot! Dear old Pressan will never change.

FRANCIS. Places sometimes look different when one comes back to them. . . . However, we'll go there together and you shall judge for yourself.

ALAN. That's ripping! My word, won't they be delighted to see you!

FRANCIS. Yes, I can just picture Hotham's face; streaming with tears of joy. And the dear Vicar.

ALAN. You sound as if you didn't like them much.

FRANCIS. Perhaps I don't.

ALAN. What a queer sort of chap you are, Francis! I can't make you out at all. You're not a bit like I imagined you would be. . . . You must have led a funny sort of life, all these years. Did you often go out by yourself, like last night?

FRANCIS. Not often, no. I had to be very careful. The last few weeks I've been more reckless, because I knew you'd catch me sooner or later. In fact, I was considering whether I oughtn't to reveal myself. It was selfish of me not to, I know; but I've enjoyed our trip so much I didn't want it to end. . . . That reminds me, here are your shoes. I always had to borrow them. You can't wear shoes in this skin, you see.

152

VOICES OF THE WAITERS *are heard singing, off.*

For in Nineveh Hotel the most humble guest ... *etc.*

ALAN.

Great God! I quite forgot! Francis, I'm in the most
awful fix! They're coming to arrest me for not pay-
ing my bill. Whatever shall I do?

FRANCIS.

Don't worry. I'd thought of that. Here, get into
the dog's skin. I'll manage the rest.

[*He helps* ALAN *to put on the dog's skin. Enter
the* MANAGER, *with* POLICEMEN, WAITERS,
etc.]

FRANCIS. Waiter, I've lost my way. How do I get to
the Roof Garden?

WAITER. Take the lift on the right, sir.

At the Fifth you alight, sir.

[*Bows.*]

MANAGER [*seeing* DOG]. That ugly brute!

I've an itch in my foot!

[*Kicks it.*]

This is the door, officer.

ALAN [*rubbing himself with his paw, in a low voice to*
FRANCIS]. The swine!

FRANCIS. Ha ha! Now you know how it feels!

POLICE SERGEANT [*at bedroom door*].

Open this door

In the name of the Law!

[*Knocks.*]

FRANCIS [*in a low voice to* ALAN]. We'll try and find
your two Journalist friends and take them with us

153

to Pressan. They may as well see how this business ends.

[*Exeunt* FRANCIS *and* ALAN.]
[*The* MANAGER, WAITERS, POLICEMEN *all stand round the door. The* POLICEMAN *knocks for the second time.*]

CURTAIN

CHORUS

So, under the local images your blood has conjured,
We show you man caught in the trap of his terror, de-
    stroying himself.
From his favourite pool between the yew-hedge and the
    roses, it is no fairy-tale his line catches
But grey, white and horrid, the monster of his childhood
    raises its huge domed forehead
And death moves in to take his inner luck,
Lands on the beaches of his love, like Coghlan's coffin.

Do not speak of a change of heart, meaning five hundred
    a year and a room of one's own,
As if that were all that is necessary. In these islands
    alone there are some forty-seven million hearts,
    each of four chambers:
You cannot avoid the issue by becoming simply a com-
    munity digger,
O you who prattle about the wonderful Middle Ages:
    You who expect the millenium after a few trifling
    adjustments.

Visit from house to house, from country to country:
    consider the populations

Beneath the communions and the coiffures: discover
your image.

Man divided always and restless always: afraid and un-
able to forgive:

Unable to forgive his parents, or his first voluptuous
rectal sins,

Afraid of the clock, afraid of catching his neighbour's
cold, afraid of his own body,

Desperately anxious about his health and his posi-
tion: calling upon the Universe to justify his exis-
tence,

Slovenly in posture and thinking: the greater part of the
will devoted

To warding off pain from the water-logged areas,

An isolated bundle of nerve and desire, suffering alone,

Seeing others only in reference to himself: as a long-lost
mother or as his ideal self at sixteen.

Watch him asleep and waking:

Dreaming of continuous sexual enjoyment or perpetual
applause;

Reading of accidents over the breakfast-table, thinking:
'This could never happen to me.'

Reading the reports of trials, flushed at the downfall of a
fellow creature.

Examine his satisfactions:

Some turn to the time-honoured solutions of sickness
and crime: some to the latest model of aeroplane or
the sport of the moment.

Some to good works, to a mechanical ritual of giving.

1st JOURNALIST. Well, Alan, your native hamlet certainly seems to be moving with the times. From your description, I was expecting an oldest inhabitant and a prize pig.

2ND J. The last of my illusions is shattered. So this is rural England! Just another lousy racket!

ALAN. But I tell you, it never used to be like this. I simply can't understand it. Everything's different! [*He looks off-stage, through the trees.*] I say, here comes the Curate! He'll be able to tell us what's up.

FRANCIS. No. I don't want him to see us, yet. [*To the* JOURNALISTS.] You two can question him. Come along, Alan. We'll go down there, where we can watch.

> [*He and* ALAN *descend into the auditorium and take seats among the audience. Enter the* CURATE.]

JOURNALISTS [*raising their hats*]. Good day, sir. *The Thunderbolt. The Evening Moon.* Perhaps you'd care to tell us something about your interesting celebrations? We're very anxious to get the details correct. Nothing shall be printed without your approval. The articles will be ready for your O.K. before we leave here this afternoon.

CURATE [*who is evidently overworked and disgusted; finding the whole subject extremely distasteful*]. I'm not authorized to give you any information. You ought to speak to the Vicar, really: but he's very busy just now. [*Sighs and passes his hand over his eyes.*] Oh, very well, what is it you want to know?

159

[*The* JOURNALISTS *take out their notebooks.*]

1ST J. My colleague and myself very much appreciate your kindness, sir. We won't take up more of your valuable time than is absolutely necessary. . . . Who exactly, are the Lads of Pressan?

CURATE [*as if wearily repeating a lesson he has learnt*]. The Lads of Pressan is a Boy's Brigade founded by the Vicar and General Hotham. Miss Iris Crewe is Patroness and Mrs Hotham Honorary Colonel-in-Chief. The uniforms have been designed by the Vicar. Today, the Brigade is to have its first inspection by General and Mrs Hotham. The Vicar will preach a sermon on Bolshevism and the Devil. And Miss Iris Crewe will present the Standard, which will then be blessed by the Vicar. Later, there will be Field Communion, tea and athletic sports.

2ND J. Very interesting. . . . And what are the objects of this Brigade?

CURATE. Well, er. . . . The Vicar says . . . you see. . . .
  [*This subject is evidently so repugnant to him that he can hardly force himself to begin.*]

1ST J. [*helpfully*]. 'Standing outside all political parties and factions, for Church, King and State, against communism, terrorism, pacifism and other forms of international anarchy, to protect Religion and succour England in times of national crisis.' Is that right, sir?

CURATE [*surprised*]. Why, those are almost exactly the Vicar's own words? However did you know?

2ND J. It's the usual, er . . . programme. Thank you very much, sir. And now, if you'll be kind enough to show us the Press places, we won't keep you any longer.

CURATE. I should think you'd see best over there.

[*He indicates two chairs in a corner, at the front of the stage. The* JOURNALISTS *go over to them and take their seats.*]

[*Band music, of a military character, can already be heard off. Enter the* VICAR, *fussily, in a bad temper. He wears his cassock and surplice.*]

VICAR [*to* CURATE]. Ah, here you are! Whatever have you been doing? I've been looking for you everywhere. Do you expect me to attend to everything myself?

CURATE. I'm very sorry.

VICAR. It's very easy to say you're sorry. But you don't do much to show it. This is the third time I've had to reprove you this week! You seem to have no life in you, no go, no enthusiasm. I'm beginning to be very much afraid that your heart isn't in our movement!

CURATE. You're quite right, sir. It's no good our going on like this: I'd better tell you frankly. . . .

[*The band, which has been getting louder, now blares out just behind the scenes.*]

THE VICAR. Good Gracious! Here they are!

[*He runs out, to meet the others; returning almost immediately with the* GENERAL, MRS HOTHAM *and* MISS IRIS CREWE. *These four take their*

161

places on the raised platform. Crowds of villagers enter and sit down on the chairs on the stage. Finally, the Lads of Pressan, wearing a distinctive uniform, march in and form ranks just below the platform. A boy with the standard which Miss Iris Crewe *is later to present takes his place on the platform behind her chair. The chatter of the villagers is drowned by the noise of the band.*]

[*The military music ends with a flourish. Silence. The* Vicar *rises to his feet. He delivers the following sermon: beginning in his usual pulpit manner, but quickly becoming more excited, more histrionic, more daring in his gestures and poses. The final passage is wailed rather than spoken. Tears pour down his cheeks, saliva runs from his mouth: He has worked himself up into an hysterical frenzy.*]

Vicar. What was the weather on Eternity's worst day? And where was that Son of God during the fatal second: pausing before a mirror in an anteroom, or in the Supreme Presence Itself, in the middle of an awful crescendo of praise, or again, withdrawn apart, regarding pensively the unspeakable beauties of the heavenly landscape?

The divinest of books says nothing. Of the primary crises of the soul no history is ever written. Yon citizen crossing the street while the policeman holds up the traffic like the Red Sea: he leaves one curb an honest man; but, ah, quickly, Constable, handcuffs out! Roll on, you heavy lorries! He is Pharaoh! Mercifully exterminate this pest! Too late, the warning cannot be given. It's done, the poison administered, the soul infected. The other curb is reached and our John Bull, honest-seeming, unsuspected, is free to walk away, within a few years to involve widows in financial ruin or a party of school children in some frightful accident.

So, on this inconceivably more catastrophic occasion, no door banged, no dog barked. There was no alarm of any kind. But consider its importance! No judge's sentence had yet been passed. Basedow's Disease had not occurred. Love. Joy. Peace. God. No words but these. No population but angels. And after . . . the whole lexicon of sin: the sullen proletariat of hell!

What, then, of the central figure in the tragedy: First among the Sons of God? Power? No Caliph or Mikado had one grain of it. Beauty? Alcibiades beside him were extraordinarily plain. Wits? Einstein were a stammerer. But for him it was not enough. For him, nothing was enough, but the unique majority of God. That or nothing! That or (ah, had he reckoned with the dread alternative!) unqualified ruin. Alas, for us he raised the question; but the answer was to lie with another!

O, even then, when the first thought tempted, was all irrevocably lost? Was there not still time, wonderful creature, to cast it from you with a phew of disgust? It doesn't matter now. Altered for ever and for the worse, he went out to corrupt others, to form his notorious and infamous societies. Gone for ever was the frank handshake, the obvious look, the direct and simple speech. The Golden Age was definitely over. Language had become symbolic, gesture a code of signals. The arrangement of books on a table conveyed a shame-faced message: flowers in a vase expressed some unsavoury *double entendre*. Personalities acquired a new and sinister significance, lost all but that. For or against: On this side of the ledger or on that. Gabriel and Michael: Out of the question. What glorious praise! Demagorgan: Safe. What a shameful comment! Abdiel and Azazael: Perhaps. Oh, beware, you unsuspecting pair! This is a terrible examination, decisive of your everlasting career. This is your only chance. There are but two colours for you to choose, the whitest white or the blackest black; salvation or damnation at one hundred per cent. Azazael chooses. What? The Black. Miserable, unlucky he! He's failed. Now, Abdiel! You hesitate? Quick, man, the White! Bravissimo, he passes ! Baffled, they slink away to make their preparations. Too late for diplomacy or apologetic telegrams. It is war.

On the details of that appalling combat, History is mercifully silent. To the vanquished, unable to consider such reminiscences without a shudder, the subject is tabu: And the victors, to whom all boasting is by nature abhorrent, have been content to leave the matter in a decent obscurity. Remember, they were divine, and therefore omniscient, omni-potent. No new-fangled auxiliary arms, the value of which is realised only by the few enthusiastic subalterns, no depth-charges or detectors, no camouflage, no poison-gas which in times of peace even generals do not see how they could bring themselves to use, no technique of deployment or barrage can have been unknown to them. It was conflict on an astronomical scale and with the gloves off. Here were no Quakers, strikers or International Red Cross, no questions of colonies or reparations. Where all were committed absolutely, there could be no ironic misgivings.

Every schoolboy knows the result. To the rebels it was destruction. The reservoirs of the Divine Wrath were inexhaustible. Nothing was signed. There was no one left to discharge so unnecessary an office. Into the fosse of Hell they fell like water. Hurrah! Hurrah! Hurrah!

Yet, my friends, you know and I know, don't we, that the events I have just narrated were not the last. Would God they had been! The scene of operations was transferred to another front, to us. Impotent to attack Him directly, the defeated sought to strike at God through His creatures, to wound, where it was most tender, His artist's love. And, to our shame, they succeeded. The world became an everlasting invalid. Of course, God could have dismissed us with a snap of His fingers. One little stellar collision and . . . no more trouble for him. Why not? All reason was for it. It would have been quite cricket. But God is no eugenist. There was no talk of sterilisation, euthanasia. Only the treatment of a very merciful and loving physician. He set over us a kindly strictness, appointed His authorities, severe but just, a kind of martial law. He gave them power to govern in His name and access to His presence in their prayers, to make their reports and ask for help and guidance, that through them the people might learn His primary will.

And so, today, we are here for a very good reason. His enemies have launched another offensive, on the grandest scale, perhaps, that this poor planet of ours has ever witnessed. As on the first awful occasion in Eden, so now: under the same deluding banner of Freedom. For their technique of propaganda has never varied; it has been far too successful for them to need to change it, to suggest that it is in the human interest to destroy God. In silk-clad China or the naked archipelagos, in the Bermudas or Brighton, in the stone hamlet among the beechwoods or the steel flats of the metropolis, that three-syllable whisper: 'You are God', has been, is and, alas, will be sufficient to convert in an instant the chapped-handed but loyal ploughboy, the patient sufferer from incurable disease, the tired economical student or the beautiful juvenile mama into a very spiteful maniac indeed, into whose hands modern science has placed an all-too-efficient axe.

166

I should like just to try and imagine for one moment what the world would be like if this lunacy with its grim fanatic theories were to spread over the civilised globe. I tell you there would exist a tyranny compared with which a termite colony would seem dangerously lax. No family love. Sons would inform against fathers, cheerfully send them to the execution cellars. Mothers send their daughters to the mines. No romance. Even the peasant must beget that standard child under laboratory conditions. Motherhood would be by licence. Truth and Beauty would be proscribed as dangerously obstructive. To be beautiful would be treason against the State, Thought a sabotage deadly to the thinker. No books, no art, no music. A year of this, I say, and even the grass would cease to grow, flowers would not risk appearance, heifers would not dare to calve.

So you see our job. To those to whom danger in God's cause makes exclaim, like a schoolboy comforted with an ice: 'How lush!' this is a lucky day. God has given them extraordinary privileges, but if there be any doubters, cowards wavering like to cowl on an oast-house, to these I say: 'Go out of that door before it is too late!' Only those whose decisions are swift as the sirocco, senses keen as the finest mirror galvanometer, will constant as the standard inch and of a chemical purity need apply. And to these I say: 'Remember, God is behind you: Nelson, Henry the Fifth, Shackleton, Julius

Caesar.' As for the enemy, those rats! they shall skedaddle like a brook; Nature herself is on our side. Their boasts are vain. You cannot threaten a thunderstorm with a revolver. They shall be trapped by the stalks of flowers. Sheep shall chase them away. Useless for them to imitate natural objects: a boulder or a tree. Even the spade-handed moles shall declare their folly!

But mind, God first! To God the glory and let Him reward! God is no summer tourist. We're more than scenery to Him. He has a farmer's eye for ergot and tares. Oh delight higher than Everest and deeper than the Challenger Gulf! His commodores come into His council and His lieutenants know His love. Lord, I confess ! I confess! I am all too weak and utterly unworthy. There is no other want. All actions and diversions of the people, their greyhound races, their football competitions, their clumsy acts of love, what are they but the pitiful, maimed expression of that entire passion, the positive tropism of the soul to God?

Oh Father, I am praising Thee, I have always praised Thee, I shall always praise Thee! Listen to the wooden sabots of Thy eager child running to Thy arms! Admit him to the fairs of that blessed country where Thy saints move happily about their neat, clean houses under the blue sky! O windmills, O cocks, O clouds and ponds! Mother is waving from the tiny door! The quilt is turned down in my beautiful blue and gold room! Father, I thank

168

Thee in advance! Everything has been grand! I am coming home!

> [*At the end of the sermon, the* VICAR *collapses like a wet rag into his chair and feebly mops his face with a handkerchief. There is a moment's silence: then a flourish of bugles.*]

THE BOY IN COMMAND OF THE LADS OF PRESSAN. Lads! Atten-shun! Eyes . . . right!

> [*The* GENERAL *and* MRS HOTHAM *come down from the platform. The* GENERAL *is in uniform with rows of medals. His wife wears a uniform jacket and a hat with an immense white plume. They begin to inspect the Lads. Fife and drum music.*]

MILDRED LUCE [*suddenly appearing from the crowd of villagers, and addressing the Lads*]. I hope you know why you're really here? The Vicar daren't tell you! The General daren't tell you either! But I dare! Wave your dummy rifles about! It's only play now. But soon they'll give you real rifles. You'll learn to shoot. You'll learn to kill whoever they tell you to. And you'll be trained to let yourselves be killed, too. I thought I'd just tell you. It isn't that I care. I'm glad! What does it matter to me if you're all murdered? My sons were murdered, and they were bigger and stronger and handsomer than you'll ever be, any of you! So what do I care!

> [*This speech has made the most painful impression on all present.* MRS HOTHAM *hurriedly leads* MILDRED *off into the background and re-*

169

turns without her. People begin talking in under-
tones. The GENERAL *abruptly cuts short the re-*
view, salutes and reascends the platform. As
people still continue to whisper, he clears his
throat angrily and rings a little handbell for si-
lence.]

GENERAL. Hrrmm! Before, er, passing on to the, er, next stage in the proceedings, I should like to say how very favourably Mrs Hotham and myself have been impressed by the excellent turn-out this after-noon.

The Lads of Pressan have made a first-rate be-ginning, and I hope that their end will be equally satisfactory . . . hrrrmm! That is, er, I should say, I hope that they will go on as they have begun.

And now I come to an important announcement. I suppose that, by this time, it's a more or less open secret that our Patroness, Miss Iris Crewe, is en-gaged to be married to that well-known munitions manufacturer, hrrmm, I should say: that well-known and popular patriot and sportsman, Mr Rudolf Trunnion-James. I'm sure we all wish her the very best of good fortune . . . hrrmm! of happi-ness.

Miss Crewe now authorises me to tell you that, after her marriage, she intends to present the Honey-pot Hall Estate to the Lads of Pressan, as barracks, parade-ground and playing-fields . . . .Three cheers for our benefactress: Miss Iris Crewe!

[*The villagers give three cheers.*]
170

ALAN [*from the auditorium*]. Here! I say!

GENERAL [*evidently fearing another interruption, tries to ignore* ALAN]. Miss Crewe's marriage has been fixed for the first day of next month, and I'm sure we all. . . .

ALAN. Shame!

THE GENERAL [*ringing his bell, continues*]. And I'm sure we all hope. . . .

ALAN. Stop! You've got to listen to me!

GENERAL. Confound it, sir! Can't you hear me speaking? Who the devil are you?

ALAN. Alan Norman.

> [*Sensation.* ALAN *gets up from his place in the auditorium and comes on to the stage.*]

ALAN. Iris, what does this mean?

IRIS [*unpleasantly surprised*]. Alan! Why have you come back?

ALAN. Because I've found Francis. [*Calling down to* FRANCIS.] Francis, come up here!

> [*Huge sensation.* FRANCIS *comes up on to the stage.*]

IRIS. Oh, dear! I feel so ill!

> [*She sways slightly in her chair and is supported by* MRS HOTHAM, *who regards* FRANCIS *with unconcealed disapproval.*]

VICAR AND GENERAL [*together: equally dismayed*]. Sir Francis! Upon my soul!

FRANCIS. Joy seems to have been too much for my dear sister's delicate constitution. . . . Hullo, General: fight back those unmanly tears! Vicar, you needn't kiss me if you don't want to. [*Looking round.*] Isn't *anybody* pleased to see me?

LITTLE GIRL [*in crowd*]. Oh, I'm awfully glad you're back: Dear old Doggy!

FRANCIS. Thank you for those kind words.

> [*Shakes hands with her.*]
>
> [*Everybody now becomes aware of the dog's skin which* FRANCIS *is wearing. There are murmurs of:*]
>
> Just fancy! The Dog! He was the dog! *etc etc.*

FRANCIS. Yes, ladies and gentlemen. The little girl is right. I am, or rather was, the Dog! [*Looking round at them.*] You know, I've often pictured to myself this very moment: My return. In fact, during my canine days, it was one of my greatest pleasures. Of course, I imagined a very dramatic appearance: tearing off my disguise and denouncing you all in the kind of language to which the vicar has just so generously treated us. But the really fascinating problem was to decide *when* to appear, and I kept putting it off. Of course, I thought, it must be just at a time when you were all cursing me and wishing I was dead. But though in private you said things about me which made my ears tingle (perhaps it did me good, too), in public you were very discreet. It was always, 'poor Sir Francis', 'good Sir Francis', 'our wonderful lost boy squire'. And now here you all are, looking extremely uncomfortable, as well you may, considering that you know I've had a dog's-eye view of you for the last ten years.

172

Directly after that historic row with my father (I forget exactly what it was about; I think it was the key of the gun-room), I went upstairs to have a hot bath, feeling very injured of course, meditating suicide, running away to sea, being brought back to die of consumption, etc. And it was in the bathroom that suddenly I had the brilliant fatal idea. An hour later, my life as a dog had begun.

At first I only intended to keep my new shape for a week or two. I even doubted if I could hold out as long as that, but I had begun to keep a diary, and that helped me over the difficult period. After the first six months I didn't really want to come back. You see, I had begun to regard you in a new light. I was fascinated and horrified by you all. I thought such obscene, cruel, hypocritical, mean, vulgar creatures had never existed before in the history of the planet, and that it was my office and doom to record it. As a dog, I learnt with what a mixture of fear, bullying, and condescending kindness you treat those whom you consider your inferiors, but on whom you are dependent for your pleasures. It's an awful shock to start seeing people from underneath.

My diary was my greatest friend. I worked away at it, like a scientist, polishing, punctuating, searching for the exact epithet, devoting months and even years to each one of you, noting every gesture, every intonation. I even managed to take photographs to illustrate my records, and very remarkable some of them are.

And then, slowly, the horror and the pseudo-scientific interest began to wear off, too. I was growing older. I began to feel that I had been foolishly wasting my time. Hadn't it all been just a romantic escape, I asked myself? Wasn't it Life itself I was afraid of, hiding in my dog-skin? I think that, soon, I should have gone away anyhow. But, as it happened, Alan Norman was chosen. I'd always liked him and so I took the opportunity of leaving you when I did.

Don't be alarmed, I haven't come back to claim my lawful rights. Iris, you can keep Honeypot Hall and do what you like with it. I never meant to return at all. Anyhow, it wasn't necessary: you are all just as I imagined you would be. Since I've been away from you, I've come to understand you better. I don't hate you any more. I see how you fit into the whole scheme. You are significant, but not in the way I used to imagine. You are units in an immense army: most of you will die without ever knowing what your leaders are really fighting for or even that you are fighting at all. Well, I am going to be a unit in the army of the other side: but the battlefield is so huge that it's practically certain you will never see me again. We are all of us completely unimportant, so it would be very silly to start quarrelling, wouldn't it? Goodbye.

[*He turns to go.*]

ALAN. Francis! I'm coming with you!

FRANCIS. I'm glad.

174

IRIS. Alan!

ALAN. I know who my friends are . . . and when I'm not
wanted.

GENERAL. This is monstrous!

CURATE. Alan, I just want to say . . . .

[*He hesitates.*]

ALAN. Come with us, too!

VICAR. You're lost if you do!

[*The* CURATE *hesitates between them, in great
distress.*]

CURATE.   Christ crucified
Be at my side,
Confirm my mind
That it be kind
To those who assert and hurt
On either side!

I must go away,
I must go to pray
To One who is greater.

GENERAL.   Greater than who?

CURATE.   Greater than you.

[*He goes out.*]

A YOUNG MAN. Francis, I'll come!

[*He crosses the stage to* FRANCIS' *side.*]

A BOY FROM THE RANKS OF THE LADS OF PRESSAN.
Let me come too, Francis!

FRANCIS. We're not going on a treasure-hunt, you
know, or looking for pirates.

175

BOY. I don't care. I want to help.

FRANCIS. All right. [*The* BOY *crosses stage.*] Any more?
    [*Three other villagers silently join the group.*]

VICAR. If anyone else thinks of joining this mistaken young man, I can only warn them that I shall make it my business to see that never, at any future time, shall he or she receive employment in Pressan again.

FRANCIS [*to his followers*]. You hear what the Vicar says? Hadn't you better go back? [*Nobody moves.*] Come on, then, let's be moving.
    [FRANCIS, ALAN *and their five companions come down from the stage and go out through the audience.*]

MRS HOTHAM.
    Reginald! Can't you say something to make them feel ashamed of themselves?

GENERAL [*shouting after them*]. You're traitors to Pressan!

FRANCIS [*turning at the auditorium exit, shouts back*]. Traitors to *your* Pressan, General: not to ours!
    [*He goes out, followed by the others.*]
    [*On the stage, everybody is talking.*]

GENERAL. That young man's a disgrace to his class and his family!

IRIS [*weeping*]. Oh dear, I've never been so insulted in all my life!

MRS HOTHAM. One can only be thankful that his poor Father isn't alive to see it!

176

VICAR [*burying his face in his hands*]. What a fiasco! What a scandal for Pressan! It was like a nightmare! I simply can't believe it has happened!

1ST JOURNALIST [*briskly coming forward*]. You're quite right, sir! It hasn't happened!

ALL. Hasn't happened? Whatever does he mean? We saw it, it must have happened!

2ND J. I entirely agree with my colleague. Dozens of things occur every day, curious, embarrassing, shocking incidents: but how few of them happen! The Press disregards them: therefore they cannot have taken place! The Press is an Artist: It has a certain picture to paint. Whatever fails to harmonise with that picture, it discards; regretfully perhaps, but firmly.

1ST J. The Press has no use for the incident you believe yourselves to have just witnessed. It has no place in our scale of values. Long-lost Baronets do not disguise themselves as dogs; or at any rate, only for erotic reasons. The behaviour of Sir Francis Crewe falls into no artistic category which we recognize: therefore it cannot be represented in our picture of the day's events.

2ND J. And since all events are recorded by the Press, what the Press does not record cannot be an event.

1ST J. But you, sir, and you, General, and you, Madam, you belong to our picture: These lads here, these flags, this charming old-world garden, they compose admirably. Allow me. Thank you. If you'll be so kind.

177

[*Talking very fast, they erect their cameras and manoeuvre the somewhat bewildered* GENERAL, VICAR *and ladies into a compact group, ready to be photographed.*]

2ND J. All ready, please.

[*There is a puff of vapour and a flash so blinding that all four cover their faces with their hands. But only for an instant. Then they recover their ceremonial poses. And now, all are masked: The* GENERAL *as a Bull, the* VICAR *as a Goat,* IRIS *as a Cat and* MRS HOTHAM *as a Turkey. They stand thus for some moments in tableau. Loud martial music. The curtain falls quickly and rises again at once. Now all the villagers wear various animal masks. The* GENERAL *is addressing them, but only a bellowing is audible. His hearers respond with various animal noises, barking, mewing, quacking, grunting, or squeaking, according to their characters. Gestures and cries become more incoherent, bestial and fantastic, until at last all are drowned in deafening military chords. The* JOURNALISTS *leave the stage through the auditorium, chatting.*]

CURTAIN

178

EPILOGUE

SEMI-CHORUS I. Love, loath to enter
The suffering winter
Still willing to rejoice
With the unbroken voice
At the precocious charm
Blithe in the dream
Afraid to wake, afraid
To doubt one term
Of summer's perfect fraud,
Enter and suffer
Within the quarrel
Be most at home,
Among the sterile prove
Your vigours, love.

SEMI-CHORUS II.

Mourn not for these; these are ghosts who chose their pain,

Mourn rather for yourselves; and your inability to make up your minds

Whose hours of self-hatred and contempt were all your majesty and crisis,

Choose therefore that you may recover: both your charity and your place

179

Determining not this that we have lately witnessed:
    but another country
Where grace may grow outward and be given praise
Beauty and virtue be vivid there.

SEMI-CHORUS I.

Where time flows on as chalk stream clear
And lovers by themselves forgiven
The whole dream genuine, the charm mature
Walk in the great and general light
In their delight a part of heaven
Its furniture and choir.

CHORUS.

To each his need: from each his power.